AUTHOR

CLASS

TITLE

The Coarse
Acting Show 2

(Further Plays for Coarse Actors)

Michael Green

Samuel French – London
New York—Sydney—Toronto—Hollywood

THE COARSE ACTING SHOW 2

INTRODUCTION

In the previous volume, *Four Plays for Coarse Actors* (*The Coarse Acting Show*), also published by Samuel French Ltd, I asked: "What are Coarse Actors and why write plays for them?" Since it took about 3,000 words to answer that question I can hardly repeat all I said then, so for those who don't know what Coarse Acting is, I'll refer them to my book *The Art of Coarse Acting*. Here are several definitions of a Coarse Actor, such as:

> One who knows when to come on stage but not where.
> One who knows everyone else's lines but not his own.
> One who addresses the scenery instead of the audience.

There are other qualities too numerous to repeat, but one infallible sign of Coarse Acting is that no matter what has gone wrong with a show—such as the collapse of a set or the failure of someone to appear on stage—the cast firmly believe no-one noticed. "The audience didn't notice a thing" is the hallmark of Coarse Drama, as is the firm belief that every show was "much better than they did it in the West End" (or on Broadway).

Coarse Theatre may be seen flourishing not only in church halls and community centres but at respectable Little Theatres and even at famous professional theatres sometimes. A Coarse Cast do not always have trouble with their lines, but if they don't they will have trouble with something else; whether it be the props, the characterization, or a scenery door which refuses to open.

Then there is Coarse Direction (or production), revealed by ghastly groupings and cliché moves (as in the Shakespeare history I saw where the King never spoke without jumping on to a rostrum). There is also Coarse Stage Management, which may force itself to the attention of the audience by a curtain which moves four feet and then sticks. A Coarse Stage Manager can turn the most serious piece of drama into Coarse Theatre, which is why good actors and actresses sometimes get caught up in it. As at a London production of *Tamburlaine the Great* when the wheels of the chariot drawn by the four degraded kings jammed on the line "Forward to Persepolis, ho . . .!" For some seconds the kings struggled without effect, and then the famous actor playing Tamburlaine resolved the situation by hissing "Stop pulling and lift the bastard . . ." There are many similar occurences which show that the baleful influence of Coarse Theatre can penetrate to the very pinnacles of drama.

These four plays, like those in *Four Plays for Coarse Actors*, are written to display various aspects of Coarse Theatre. If anyone said they were spoofs of amateur dramatics I wouldn't disagree, except that they are also spoofs of some professional dramatics too. They were taken to the 1979 Edinburgh Festival as a sequel to the original 1977 *Coarse Acting Show* under the title of *The Coarse Acting Show 2*, and performed by the same company from the Questors' Theatre, Ealing. After the Festival, Brian Rix selected four Fringe shows to go to the Shaftesbury Theatre, London, for a six-week season under the general title *Lunatic Fringe*, and *The Coarse Acting Show 2* was one of these. This was the first official appearance of Coarse Acting in the West End, although unofficially they've had it for years. H.R.H. Prince Charles was kind enough to see one performance, and proved how universal Coarse Acting is by telling the cast of an experience of his own, when the school music master was asked to direct *Richard III* and did so in the style of Gilbert and Sullivan with disastrous results.

The deliberately staged version of Coarse Acting has now been around since the original World Coarse Acting Championship was held to raise funds for the Questors' Theatre at Ealing in 1972, and a certain amount of experience has been gained. The first lesson we have learned is the need for sincerity. It is not a competition in hamming it up. Really, Coarse Acting is a representation of a company struggling to do their best and being defeated. In real life most Coarse Actors would indignantly deny they were Coarse. They are trying hard, it's just that the scenery keeps falling down, or the sound cues are all wrong, or they chose the wrong play. Earnest incompetence is the keynote.

Nothing kills the humour in a Coarse Acting show more quickly than overdoing it. Understatement is far funnier. A flicker of the eyes is often enough to convey the predicament. Over-acting is just embarrassing. This also applies to the technical side. The lights and sound don't want to be wrong *all* the time. It is far funnier if they nearly get it right with occasional spectacular lapses.

A production doesn't need to be *all* Coarse. There must be some straight background to provide contrast. If in doubt about directing one of the plays in this book, start straight and go from there, rather than begin with everyone sending up the whole thing. If everything is going wrong all the time the play stops being funny.

I find it helps sometimes to ask: What would a bad director do here? We used to discuss the question among the cast and it is surprising what ingenious ideas come out, such as the horrible moment in *The Cherry Sisters* when Footrotski and the Stationmaster both turn and retire up stage in perfect unison—one of those supremely artificial moves which are the trademark of the bad director. The same technique can be applied to props, wardrobe or any backstage department. It was through asking ourselves what a bad wardrobe department would do that Ishmael got a costume so small he could only move with difficulty.

It may seem rather pretentious to analyse the humour in a Coarse Play but there are several layers. One strand is the predicament of people who are trying to do something they are incompetent at, such as poor Footrotski in *The Cherry Sisters*, who is one of those non-actors who stands up every time he speaks, and delivers his lines in a monotone. But equally important is the situation of those who can act to some extent but who are defeated by external circumstances, such as the leak which develops in the samovar in the same play. Another aspect was represented by Lorna Duval when she played Veruka at the Shaftesbury Theatre. It was a performance of great sincerity—perhaps rather over-intense but desperately sincere—as it might have been given by Mrs Venables, the chairman's wife. Only one thing marred it—she played it with a speech defect that caused her to shower spit over the other characters every time she spoke the letter "s".

Another level of humour is represented by the stock characterizations of the Coarse Actor, revealed in old men such as Elijah in *Moby Dick* or villains like Wolverhampton in *Henry the Tenth*. A further strand of humour lies in the pastiche element of the plays themselves, which are written to exaggerate certain characteristics of the original authors, especially those which have become almost clichés, such as Shakespeare's battle scenes and Chekov's long silences. So some plays are best done almost straight (although always with the tongue in the cheek). Others can take a broader treatment. Thus, any Coarse Play contains many elements, not the least of which is the sense of burlesque of the original. A good example is *The Cherry Sisters* where in Footrotski we have a non-actor playing opposite one or two others who (almost) get there. On the other hand, *Streuth*, in the first *Coarse Acting Show*, had a cast of which fully half were appalling actors (including one man who read his lines from a cigarette case and another who ran all his words together), because this was a different piece of satire, aimed at a typical village-hall murder mystery production. It is important to decide who is the target of your burlesque.

It sometimes helps if the company adopt an identity and imagine themselves as (say) the Ministry of Defence Players or Lewisham Co-Operative Society Arts Club. Some of our players used to work out their positions in an imaginary group. We decided a certain actor was an unpopular little man who got all the rotten parts, while the King in Shakespeare was treasurer of the society (and a senior bank official). Naturally his wife took the female leads. The actor who played the much-abused Herald in *Henry the Tenth* played him as Old Reg, who was always being kicked around on and off stage.

Some groups give a theme to the evening, and perhaps start with an introduction by the "Vicar" or the "College Principal" together with announcements about the toilets being out of action. Watching perfor-mances of the first show (*Four Plays for Coarse Actors*) I've been very impressed by the ingenuity of directors and actors in introducing their own ideas. I hope they won't hesitate to do the same with this collection, although the plays don't need a stream of gimmicks to help them along.

What a pity, though, that some directors omit essential business because it's difficult. I have seen *Moby Dick* done without Ahab's absurd wooden leg, which is the whole comic focus.

Incredible though it may seem, some people don't realize Coarse Acting shows are designed to go wrong. Like the old dear who said, "I liked the plays very much but I didn't think the acting was very good." So try to give some idea of what it is all about in the programme.

Just a word on casting. The enormous numbers of characters in the script can be shaved down with judicious doubling (which is a hallmark of Coarse Theatre, anyway). Some scenes and characters can be cut, of course. The professional Gemini Company, of Dublin, actually achieved the miracle of doing the show with a cast of six (plus help from stage staff). Not that one would recommend this. The more like a genuine production the plays are, the better.

The above are general tips on tackling the show, and individual advice for each play is given in the production notes. But one final warning: THESE PLAYS ARE DANGEROUS. It takes a good actor to mimic a bad one. The plays have been proved to be funny when they work, but like so much comedy they rest on a razor's edge and a cast which can't cope will be embarrassingly unamusing. Even a cast which *can* cope will be equally unfunny if they go over the top. Unfortunately Coarse Acting works like a drug on a cast and a director will find he (or she) will have to work hard to keep the cast under control as a run goes on. Which just proves we are all Coarse Actors at heart.

The plays are given here in what I believe to be the best order of performance:

1. *Moby Dick*
2. *The Cherry Sisters*
3. *Last Call For Breakfast*
4. *Henry the Tenth* (*Part Seven*)

When the plays were performed at Edinburgh and in the West End, however, for technical reasons the order was: *Moby Dick*; *Last Call*; *Cherry Sisters*; *Henry the Tenth*.

Some groups may find part of the programme is difficult or unsuitable for their audiences. I would suggest in that case making a combined show of plays from *Four Plays For Coarse Actors*, which is the published version of the first *Coarse Acting Show*, and this volume. A good programme would be: *Moby Dick*; *The Cherry Sisters*; *Streuth*; *Henry the Tenth*.

The principal authors of each piece are given but most of them contributed to each other's work. The authors are all members of the Coarse Acting Company from the Questors' and I am also grateful to other members of the cast who contributed their ideas. I am especially grateful to Michael Langridge, associate director, for his help and suggestions.

Michael Green

CREDITS

Normally, published plays list the original cast but not the stage staff and technical crew. This always seems a little unfair to me. In any case, ninety per cent of the Coarse Acting Company backstage workers appeared on stage, glued to the back of a collapsing flat, as an arm handing in a prop or moving the tortuous scenery. Even the front-of-house manager was pressed in to wipe the fore-stage after the watery ending to *The Cherry Sisters* (she usually got the best applause of the evening). In Coarse Theatre, the lighting and sound crews too, have a specially big role to play in creating the show and may give as much amusement to the audience as the actors and actresses (more, says a friend bitterly). So here is a list of our technical and backstage crew as an acknowledgement of the part they played:

Stage Manager	Lesley Montgomery
Deputy Stage Manager	Alec Atchison
Assistant Stage Managers	Phil Dean, Vicki Gaunt, Chris Lejeune, Nina Robinson
Lighting Designer	Pete Walters, assisted by Sue Kendrick
Sound	Colin Horne, assisted by Elaine Stanley
Props	Beth Crowley
Wardrobe	Grace Lacaille
Construction	Phil Dean, Geoff Moore, Bob Ricket
Transport	Richard Lewis
Prompt	Monique Fare
Business Manager	Richard Johnson
General Staff	Chris Sydenham, Rita Fenoughty, Carole Begent

MOBY DICK

MOBY DICK

By Michael Green and Michael Langridge

(Grateful acknowledgement is made to the Southampton Maskers Company for the use of certain material)

First performed at the George Square Theatre, Edinburgh, on August 20th 1979, and subsequently at the Shaftesbury Theatre, London, with the following cast:

Ishmael	Michael Langridge
Landlady, an old crone	Anne Johnson
Starbuck	John Turner
Queequeg	Robin Duval
Preacher	Richard Lewis
Elijah	Tony Worth
Ahab	David Pearson
Carpenter	Brian Pickles
Seamen	Paul Collins, Richard Gaunt, Richard Johnson, Richard Lewis, Tony Worth
Serving Wenches, Inhabitants of Nantucket, etc.	Lorna Duval, Anne Johnson, Sonia Pearson, John Stacey, Maggie Turner

The play directed by Michael Green

Setting by John Stacey

(Herman Melville wrote the novel *Moby Dick*. It is 685 pages long)

PRODUCTION NOTES

The essence of *Moby Dick* is the sheer audacity of a small and not very good group tackling this vast epic (the novel is 685 pages long) and reducing it to a series of quick-fire scenes. This over-ambition is typical of Coarse Theatre. I feel *Moby Dick* might well be the product of a teachers' training college with a director who wanted to impress the Principal and a script written by a lecturer in English who fancied himself as a writer.

The prime essential in producing the show is pace. Pace above all. It must whip along at great speed, since half the fun is the absurd way in which events follow one another. Ishmael, the narrator, is a key character. Our Ishmael played him as a man who had learned his acting from a book. Almost every word was enlivened with a stock gesture or a pointing finger (usually in the wrong direction). He was hampered by a costume which was too small. An appalling false American accent caused him to emphasize all the wrong words, so his opening lines went something like this: "Call *me* Ishmael; some years ago having little or *no* money *I* thought *I* would sail about and *see* the oceans of *the* world . . ."

The crew and the other all-purpose characters represent total Coarse cliché. They are the archetypal Coarse Chorus, waving cardboard beer mugs and revealing the hand of an unimaginative director in every stilted move (see any amateur production of *The Student Prince*). They continually react in unison to whatever anybody else is saying, and punctuate dialogue with meaningless cries of "Aaaaah, uuurgh, oh ho", etc., because this is how they believe stage seamen ought to behave (for examples listen to the crowd in a BBC radio production). Props and costumes reflect the acting. Southampton Maskers gave everyone two-dimensional beer mugs; our beer mugs had plastic foam which fell off. We gave them all eye-patches on the principal that all Coarse seamen are blind in one eye ("Got to get some character into the part, old chap . . ."). There's no reason why the serving-girls shouldn't have eye-patches as well.

Elijah and Queequeg are similar stock performances. Queequeg may be based on something from *The Black and White Minstrel Show* or not, according to taste. Elijah looks like an advert for sardines.

Ahab is a sad figure. One feels he can probably act a little in a rather hammy way and this was his big opportunity. Unfortunately, his efforts are ruined by a badly designed wooden leg, four inches too short, which he cannot control. Needless to say he didn't receive it until the dress rehearsal, so there has been no time for practice or alteration, and he simply lurches about the stage trying to keep his balance.

Ken Spencer, who master-minded the original version by Southampton Maskers, says it was first conceived as a multi-media production with slides, film, back projection and so forth. This idea was later dropped but it seems a good suggestion if facilities are available, and gives great scope for things to go wrong. Corny live effects are another good wheeze. I recall a school play in which waves were imitated by ten small boys crouched underneath a stage-cloth. We toyed with using the idea but did not have ten expendable little boys. But any gimmicks must be the sort of thing a real production might have. Authenticity is all-important.

Don't skimp the whale. It should be huge and two-dimensional. We had four operators—three in the front and one in the back. The more bits that move, such as eye, jaw, etc., the better. For a spout, a spray of powder may be found more effective than water. The whale must completely hide the operators, except for their feet twinkling underneath. Actors not on stage can be the whale's crew.

Finally, as with all Coarse Drama, remember the basis of truth. No matter what goes wrong, this must still remain a production of *Moby Dick*—a misplaced production, an over-ambitious disaster, but still a coherent attempt to tell the tale. Afterwards the college Principal will praise the show and ask who built the whale. And someone else will say, "I think it was even better than that version they did in the West End . . ."

(*Footnote:* The seamen's disastrous hornpipe is an important part of the deck scene. The two dancers should be holding opposite ends of a length of rope and dance traditional hornpipe steps round each other in a figure-of-eight pattern, so that they become completely bound up in the rope and can hardly move, although they struggle to continue the dance. Music is at the director's discretion, although we simply had the rest of the crew whistling and clapping. This dance reveals the fatal hand of the dreaded Mrs Venables, wife of the society chairman.)

MOBY DICK

A bare stage, except for an inn-sign for the "Try Pots Inn". Warmers light the stage while the House Lights are up

The National Anthem is jerkily played in fits and starts on what sounds like a thirty-year-old record. The House Lights fade, and the introductory music starts. This is something stirring but not quite right, such as the theme from "Star Wars" or Mendelssohn's "Fingal's Cave". As the music swells to a climax, the warmers snap out and are replaced by a blinding follow-spot. Unfortunately, Ishmael, whom the Spot is supposed to pick up, is not there. The Spot wanders slowly over the stage searching for him and then goes out. There is the sound of a tape-recorder being played backwards, the House Lights go up and the whole process begins again

As the House Lights come up, Ishmael, sea-bag over his shoulder, marches confidently on stage, stares horrified at the audience for a moment and then flees. Shortly afterwards, as the music draws to its end again, he is seen creeping furtively on stage in the light of the warmers (one of the more pathetic beliefs of Coarse Actors is that they can't be seen if they tip-toe). He takes up a commanding position and strikes a pose. Then he looks at his feet and decides they are not on their marks. He moves from his position to one side and strikes his pose again. After a few moments, he decides he is still not in the right position and moves again

As he stands shifting his feet uneasily, the Spot comes on, neatly bisecting him. He does not move into it, but addresses the audience with his face almost invisible

Ishmael Call me Ishmael. Some years ago, having little or no money in my purse I thought I would sail about and see the watery part of the world. It is a way I have of driving off the spleen. Whenever it is damp, drizzly November in my soul, whenever I feel like knocking people's hats off in the street, then I account it high time to get to sea again. The sea . . . the sea . . . the sea . . .

There is a sudden outbreak of sea noises. Ishmael peers into the Spot, is blinded, and retreats into darkness again

Which like a magnetic compass draws men on to it. Thus it was that I duly arrived at the whaling island of Nantucket, Massachusetts, on a stormy night late in the year eighteen forty-one.

He goes to exit one way, changes his mind, and exits in the other direction

The Spot fades and the Lights come up on the interior of the "Try Pots Inn". The Seamen enter, singing as they come, together with the Landlady and the Serving Wenches. The men all have eye-patches and look like something out of a bad production of Gilbert and Sullivan, except that they wear wellington boots and a few have strange odds and ends such as rugby shirts and donkey jackets with "Wimpey" on the back. They carry in benches and a trestle table which they have difficulty in erecting. They arrange themselves in carefully prepared positions and sing "What Shall We Do with the Drunken Sailor?" with much waving of cardboard mugs. One of them plays a fake concertina so vigorously that it breaks in two. They then break into a howl of meaningless grunts and cries

Ishmael enters and watches the scene

The Landlady, a fearsome crone of about 95, approaches him

Landlady Welcome to the *Try Pots Inn*. I am Mrs Hussey.

The Seamen interrupt her with a chorus of growls. She repeats the line with savage emphasis

Welcome to the *Try Pots Inn*. I am Mrs Hussey.
Ishmael Who are these cheery fellows, my good woman?
Landlady They're goin' whalin' in the mornin'.
Seamen Aye, whalin', in the mornin', goin' whalin'.

The trestle table collapses with a terrible crash

Ishmael I intend to offer my services if I can find a suitable berth.
Landlady You'll have to ask them.
Seamen Aye, ask us, ask us . . . *etc.*

They re-erect the table

Landlady The sea belongs to Nantucketeers, they own it as Emperors own Empires . . . other seamen only have a right of way through it.

A hideously scarred Seaman approaches. His disfigured and useless arm swings to and fro alarmingly. He sniffs at Ishmael

Scarred Seaman He don't smell like a whaling man, lads. (*To Ishmael*) You must know, whalemen always smell of sperm . . .

There is an awkward pause. Ishmael looks highly embarrassed

Ishmael (*hissing*) Oil!
Scarred Seaman Oil. Sperm-*oil*, he don't smell of sperm-*oil!*
Seamen (*relieved*) Aye, oil, oil, sperm-oil.
Scarred Seaman Are you from Nantucket?
Ishmael No, I am not from Nantucket. (*As always with difficult words he gets his tongue caught round "Nantucket"*)
Scarred Seaman Not from Nantucket and goin' whalin'?
Ishmael Yes.
Scarred Seaman Shall we take him, lads?
Seamen Aye, aye, take him.
Scarred Seaman Then let's drink to our new shipmate.

They drink with much waving of mugs. Once more the table threatens to collapse and is saved at the last minute. Ishmael crosses to the table and in doing so swings his sea-bag over his shoulder, catching the scarred Seaman on the face. He staggers back and most of his disguise falls off, including his wig, his false nose, his straggling beard, and perhaps some of his warts and scars. He also loses his contact lenses and gropes blindly on the floor. Suddenly there is a clap of thunder for no reason at all. In the ensuing silence the "thump-bang" of Ahab's artificial leg, obviously done by a stage-hand in the wings, is heard. The Seamen register fear, crossing themselves etc.

Seamen It's Ahab! Ahab!

Ishmael Who the devil is Ahab?

Starbuck Our master, Captain Ahab. Seek to know no more. But here comes the harpooneer you're to sleep with!

The Seamen growl their agreement

Queequeg enters. He is inadequately made up as a cannibal. His facial make-up finishes abruptly in a neat line round his neck; his legs are encased in black tights with holes in them; his body is covered in a black pullover; and he wears a grass skirt which is short enough to reveal the sagging crutch of his tights. His face is probably made up like Al Jolson about to sing "Mammie". He has a bone clipped to his nose as if it was piercing it. This sometimes slips off, and is replaced like a pair of spectacles or given to someone to hold. He wears a belt from which dangle tennis balls made to look like shrunken heads

Ishmael So I'm to sleep with thee?

More stage laughter from the Seamen

Queequeg Me Queequeg the cannibal.

Ishmael Well Queequeg, what is that thing dangling in front of you? (*He points at Queequeg's loins*)

Queequeg Queequeg sell shrunken heads. You wish to buy from Queequeg? (*He fiddles with his belt to show them and a head drops off, and with any luck bounces over the footlights*)

Ishmael Are you a good harpooneer, Queequeg?

Queequeg Queequeg best harpooneer in Nantucket. Me show. You see spot of tar on water outside window?

Ishmael You can't hit that, can you?

Queequeg Queequeg hit it. Me show.

He waves his harpoon wildly. Everyone flees for safety. With tremendous energy he hurls it off stage from whence there is a strangled cry of pain. A pause. Queequeg draws in his harpoon by its rope. It comes in with someone's shoe on the end of it. Another horrified pause

Ishmael Well Queequeg you've convinced me of your skill as a harpooneer.

The Seamen laugh mirthlessly, and then all, apart from Ishmael, exit, taking the props with them. As Queequeg goes, he tries to remove the shoe from his harpoon

The Lights dim. Ishmael moves to the centre of the stage and once more is expertly bisected by the Spot

How it is I know not but there is no place like bed for a confidential chat between friends. Thus, then in our heart's honeymoon, lay I and Queequeg, a cosy loving pair, Queequeg now and again affectionately throwing his long brown leg over mine . . . In the morning I experienced a desire to go to church. (*He moves across the stage, the Spot following with difficulty*) Now in this same town there stands a whaleman's chapel and few are the fishermen shortly bound for the Pacific who fail to pay it a visit.

As he speaks, the congregation enter in the half black-out, carrying a pulpit, which they position on stage. The congregation is mostly women, but hopefully includes some of the Seamen from the previous scene. They kneel

Its chaplain is Father Mapple, a famous harpooneer in his youth, who preaches from a lofty pulpit approached by a ship's rope ladder up which he climbs to deliver his sermon . . .

The Spot on Ishmael fades and the Lights come up. Ishmael joins the congregation and they sing the first verse of "Eternal Father, Strong to Save". None of them know the words except one woman whom they struggle to follow, usually one line behind. As the last notes die away, a strong Spot shines on the pulpit, and all, still kneeling, look towards it. No-one appears. There is a ghastly hiatus. All look at one another, and then sing "Eternal Father" again

During the singing, one of the women, still on her knees, goes off into the wings and returns shaking her head

There is another confused pause, broken by a woman who decides to save the situation

Woman To the Quay! To the Quay!
All (*thankfully*) Yes, to the Quayside, to the ship, to the docks, let us go, to the quay . . . *etc.*

They exit, shouting as they go, leaving Queequeg and Ishmael still kneeling and looking puzzled as this hasn't happened before. After a short pause the woman comes back and repeats her line while jerking her thumb towards the wings, where the others are beckoning, visible to the audience

Woman To the Quay! To the Quay! To the Quay! The Quay!
Ishmael } The Quay! { *Together*
Queequeg

Queequeg and Ishmael get the message and leave. The Lights fade and then come up again almost immediately, as Queequeg and Ishmael return. "Good King Wenceslas" is heard, as some of the Seamen enter, remove the pulpit, and set up bollards for the Quay scene

Ishmael Queequeg, it's Christmas Day! Shall we ever see another, here in Nantucket? Maybe we shall spend our next on your very own Pacific island of Coqo . . . Coqovo . . . Coqovin . . .

Ishmael fades away as the Preacher, who should have been in the church scene, hurries on, confidently strides to where the pulpit was, and starts to bless the congregation. He realizes there is no-one there and looks round, bewildered

Queequeg moves to him

Queequeg (*sotto voce*) Piss off!

The Preacher leaves hurriedly

Ah yes, Coqovocco ... Coqovocco ... (*He laughs maniacally and attempts a war dance which ends in disaster. Probably his grass skirt falls down*)

Elijah enters. He is dressed in a long oilskin and to hide the fact that he hasn't made up properly he wears a huge beard and sou'wester hat which reaches down to his mouth. He has a hook in place of one hand (the actor should hold the shaft of the hook in his clenched fist, covered by a sock). Nothing can be seen of his face

Elijah Avast there.

Ishmael We're just going on board the *Pequod*, we sail this morning.

Elijah The *Pequod*? The *Pequod*? (*As he says this a cloud of make-up powder explodes from his beard*) Ye have shipped in that ship?

Ishmael We have just signed articles.

Elijah Anything down there about your souls? (*He waves his hand mysteriously and the hook gets entangled with his beard. He tries to free it as he speaks*) Or perhaps ye don't know about Captain Ahab?

Ishmael What's wrong with Ahab?

Elijah Wrong? Wrong? Let this stiffened arm of mine testify what's wrong.

He eventually manages to free the hook from his beard and waves his arm like a scythe, catching the hook on Queequeg's harpoon shaft. This time it falls off and is salvaged by Ishmael

They didn't tell ye about his leg being taken off according to the prophecy?

Ishmael I know all about the loss of his leg.

Elijah And what about the loss of his soul? Mark this. Ahab sails to his doom and so do all that sail with him.

Ishmael But what is your name, old madman?

Elijah They call me ... (*He forgets his name*)

Queequeg (*prompting him, sotto voce*) Elijah!

Elijah They call me ... Jeremiah.

He begins to move off. Ishmael slips him his hook as he goes. He replaces it and exits with his stiffened arm in front of him

Ishmael Never mind him, Queequeg. This looks like the good ship, the *Queequeg*, Pequod—the *Pequeg*, Queequod ... the one we've signed for. (*He has some difficulty with this convoluted sentence*)

The side of a ship glides on. Or it can be carried by its crew. It is the

"Pequod". Ishmael and Queequeg board it and the Crew come in with a crowd of women who have come to wave the ship good-bye. Wives and sweethearts kiss rather over-enthusiastically. There is much growling and shouting and rhubarbing

Seamen All aboard! All aboard!

The shout is taken up by the crowd. The last Seamen go aboard

Starbuck Cast off fore and aft! Cast off and hoist the mainsail!

Everyone takes up the cry. The mooring ropes are cast off from the bollards on stage. All wave good-bye, cheer and weep, etc. The Seamen sing. To give the impression the ship is moving the crowd walk backwards, towing the bollards with them on string and waving vigorously

> *The Lights fade and all exit. A loud trampling sound indicates that the ship is being removed to the detriment of an actor with his face stuck in a porthole*

> *Ishmael re-enters. As he speaks, the next scene, representing the deck of the "Pequod", is set behind him (deck-rail, capstans, ropes, etc.). This time he misses the Spot completely and it pursues him round the stage. Sometimes he becomes entangled with the scene-setters*

Ishmael And so, after sailing from the little harbour, and dropping the pilot, the *Pequod* blindly plunged like fate into the lone Atlantic. How it is, there is no telling, but islanders seem to make the best whalemen. They were nearly all islanders in the *Pequod*. They came from all the isles of the sea, and the ends of the earth, and they were a lively set of lads.

The Spot on Ishmael fades, and the Lights come up

> *To a background of sea effects, the Crew enter and perform various nautical tasks with complete incompetence, pulling on ropes, turning capstans, etc. Two start a figure-of-eight hornpipe while holding a length of rope. The dance ends in disaster with both men enmeshed in rope and tied face-to-face, while the Crew clap hands in time and whistle the tune. Moving together, the entangled pair hobble to one side*

For several days after leaving Nantucket nothing above hatches was seen of Captain Ahab. It was only at night he could be heard walking the deck . . .

The thump-bang of Ahab's leg is heard off stage. All register fear

Then one day came the order we had waited for . . .

Starbuck Everybody aft! Everybody muster aft! Mast-headers come down and muster aft!

The Crew gather expectantly

> *Ahab enters, preceded by the thump of his leg. His wooden leg is just what you would expect from an amateur dramatic society. It is sewn on to the knee of his trousers, and it is four inches too short so he has difficulty in getting it to the ground at right angles. It skids in front of him as he tries*

to walk. His real leg is inadequately strapped up behind him and the foot can be seen underneath his captain's long coat. He has a crutch. For the first few moments he is totally out of control but gradually regains some sort of balance although the slightest move is fraught with danger and he clings to the proscenium arch for support

Ahab Men . . . what do ye do when ye see a whale?
Seamen We yell, Captain.
Ahab Good. And what do ye yell?
Seamen There, there she blows!
Ahab And what do ye do next, men?
Seamen Go after him.
Ahab (*starting to pace the deck precariously*) And what do ye sing?
Seamen A good whale is a dead whale.

Some of them start to sing "Drunken sailor" but are silenced

Ahab All ye mast-headers have heard me give orders about whales, a white whale especially.
Seamen White whale . . . white whale . . .
Ahab Look ye then . . . (*he produces a coin from his pocket*) . . . see this Spanish sixteen dollar gold piece . . . do ye see it? (*He nearly falls and is saved by some of the Crew*)
Seamen Aye, aye.
Ahab Whosoever raises me the white-headed whale with a crinkled brow and a crooked jaw, he that sights this whale shall have this gold ounce.
Seamen Gold ounce . . . gold ounce.
Ahab Carpenter, your maul! I'll nail it to the mast myself.

Taking the hammer from the Carpenter, Ahab turns to nail the coin to the mast, but the mast has failed to appear from the flies. Both he and the Carpenter look wildly round for it

Here, Carpenter, you do it.

The Carpenter begins an investigation about the mast

It is the white whale that I seek.
Ishmael Is that the same whale that some call—(*he turns his head to the audience*)—Moby Dick!
Ahab Aye, aye. Moby Dick.
Seamen (*also turning their heads significantly to the audience*) Moby Dick! Moby Dick!
Ahab Aye, men—Moby Dick . . . the white whale with the enormous spout . . . he fantails like a slit jib in a squall . . .
Starbuck Was it not that same Moby leg that took off thy Dick?

There is a pause. Everyone looks embarrassed. Starbuck corrects the line carefully

Was it not that same Moby Dick that took off thy leg?

Ahab Aye, it was Moby Dick that dismasted me ... Moby Dick that
brought me to this dead stump I stand on. (*He teeters about*)

*The mast appears slowly from above, hesitates a moment and then goes up
again as the Carpenter rushes towards it*

Thunder and hell! 'Twas Moby Dick that tore my body and soul until
they bled into each other. I'll chase that white whale round the oceans
of the world until he spurts black blood and rolls dead in red foam.

Several Seamen register disgust as this unpleasant description

Optional

*The following scene, down to the exit of the "Rachel", is an addition to the
original production. It has been inserted for the benefit of those who want a
longer show*

Seamen A ship! A ship!
Ahab Let me see! Let me see! (*He leaves the support of whatever he is
clinging to and hops to the rail, where he overbalances and crashes through
it. He is helped to his feet and the set is re-erected hastily*)
'Tis the good ship *Rachel*. Ahoy, *Rachel*!

The "Rachel" may appear or not as the director pleases

Voice (*off*) Ahoy, there! This is the *Rachel*. Have you seen one of our
boats?
Ahab Not a sign. Have ye seen the white whale?
All White whale, white whale.
Voice (*off*) Aye, Captain Ahab, we have, just after we parted from you
yesterday. It towed one of our boats out of sight and the Captain's little
son in it, too. Will you help us look for the boat?
All His son, his son.
Ahab (*after an inward struggle*) No. I must seek the white whale. Leave us.

All register horror of the deepest kind

Starbuck Then we are doomed, lads!
Voice (*off*) Curses on ye, Captain Ahab. May the white whale strike ye
dead!

The "Rachel" exits jerkily. End of optional scene

Ahab Come, lads, let's pledge ourselves. Get the great measure of grog!
(*He takes the grog bottle from one of the Seamen*) Now drink and pass!
Drink and pass. God hunt us all if we do not hunt Moby Dick to his
death!
Seamen (*passing the bottle round*) Aye, drink and pass, drink and pass,
Pass and drink, pass and drink ..., *etc.*

*Suddenly there is a ghastly cry from Ahab who throws away his crutch in
agony and hops wildly round the deck*

Ahab Cramp! Cramp! Oh God, my leg. Quick untie my leg!

There is a rush to help him. He is carried face-downwards to one side of the stage while one of the Crew unties his leg and massages it. Meanwhile, the rest of the Crew ad lib "Pass and drink" until Starbuck brings relief with his line

Starbuck Man overboard! Man overboard!

They all rush to the rail, leaving Ahab to collapse on the deck. A dummy hurtles from above and lands on the deck. The Crew realize the mistake, seize it and shove it overboard. There is a loud splash, followed by a cry. A hand with a cup of water appears from behind the scenery and throws water in someone's face

Seaman Not a sign of him. The sea has swallowed him up.
Starbuck Aye . . . the first victim. But not the last.

The Crew growl and register fear yet again. The Lights dim and the Spot comes up. Ishmael steps into the edge of it

Ishmael After this ill omen we were hit by a terrible storm.

Lightning and thunder. The Crew hurl themselves from side to side, imitating effects of a storm. This should be organized into a corny semi-dance routine obviously directed by Mrs Venables

And this was followed by an endless calm . . .

All cease rocking and sway gently until finally stopping, except for one who is brought into line with a savage prod of an elbow

Seamen Becalmed! Becalmed!
Ishmael It was if the Gods were warning us not to go on. But Ahab heeded no warnings. Night and day he paced the deck until one day came the cry he had waited for . . .

The Spot fades on Ishmael

Seamen Thar! Thar! Thar! Thar she blows!

Ahab, who has been crawling round the deck, lurches to his feet and staggers across to the rest of the Crew, walking on his own legs while the wooden one hangs obscenely from the knee of his trousers. The Crew are excitedly shouting and all pointing in different directions

Ahab Did you see his crooked jaw?
Seamen Aye, crooked jaw.
Ahab And did you see his snow white hump?
Seamen Yes, hump, hump.
Ahab And the glittering teeth?
Seamen Teeth. Teeth.
Ahab Then it is surely Moby Dick! I'll ten times girdle the unmeasured globe; yea and dive straight throught it, but I'll slay him yet!

The Lights dim. Stirring music plays as the deck scene is struck and the next scene is set with a certain amount of confusion. The Spot comes up on Ishmael

Ishmael And so Ahab gave the order to man the boats, and they set off to leeward in pursuit of the white whale.

The Seamen carry in their whaling boat, striking Ishmael as they pass

After a while they halted over the spot where the great beast had sounded and waited, patiently.

The Spot fades on Ishmael. The Lights come up on the Crew seated in the whaling boat, with Ahab standing in the prow with his harpoon. Two of the Crew are facing each other. Both change over so one of them is still wrong. They all row. A smaller cut-out of the "Pequod" is set at the back of the stage

Ahab Thar she blows! Thar she blows! Row lads and split your lungs!

The Whale appears. It squirts

She breeches! She breeches!

The Whale squirts again and charges Ahab, who ignores the fact that he is at sea and rushes all over the stage

Aye, breech your last to the sun, Moby Dick.

The Whale dances uncertainly about. It loses its eye and a hand gropes for it

Towards thee I roll, thou all-destroying but unconquering whale. To the last I grapple with thee. From hell's heart I stab . . . I stab . . . at thee. (*He stabs at the Whale*)

The Whale splits in half

The front part exits

Ahab attacks the rear part, which dithers uncertainly

Towards thee I roll, thou all-destroying but unconquering whale. To the last I grapple with thee. From hell's heart I stab . . . I stab . . . at thee.

The tail flees hastily off stage and exits with difficulty after first running into the scenery or some other obstruction

As Ahab looks off stage waving his harpoon the front of the Whale appears on the other side of the stage. Ahab turns on it

Towards *thee* I roll, thou all-destroying but unconquering whale. To the last I grapple with thee . . .

The head forces Ahab down stage nearly to the footlights. He desperately knocks on it and it retreats

From hell's heart I stab at thee. Thus I give up the spear. (*He stabs the Whale*)

The Whale's jaw seizes Ahab's arm and drags him off. He shouts. His shouts continue into the wings for an unnecessary length of time

Queequeg The ship! The ship! The *Pequod* is sinking!

The small cut-out of the ship stands on end

Starbuck The suction. The suction. We are going down with the *Pequod*. We are destroyed.

All The suction. The suction. We are going down with the *Pequod* . . . down . . . down . . .

The Crew leave the whaler and mime being sucked down by a whirlpool. This is another of Mrs Venables' dances, perhaps to music

The back half of the Whale enters, crosses the stage in confusion and exits on the other side

Ishmael enters. As he speaks, the back half of the Whale enters again and tip-toes about uncertainly

Ishmael The drama's done . . . the great shroud of the sea rolls over the *Pequod*, her crew and Moby Dick, and I alone escaped to tell the tale, saved from the sea by the good ship *Rachel* . . .

He turns to leave the stage but treads all over the drowned seamen. Oaths and cries are heard

Lights fade, music swells. The Lights come up suddenly to reveal everybody fighting to get into position for the curtain call

Ahab enters, his leg now strapped up, and takes a bow. He overbalances and knocks down the line. Suddenly he is assailed by cramp again. He is dragged off

THE CHERRY SISTERS

THE CHERRY SISTERS

By Michael Green, David Pearson,
Michael Langridge, Richard Gaunt and John Turner

First performed at the George Square Theatre, Edinburgh, on August 20th, 1979, and subsequently at the Shaftesbury Theatre, London, with the following cast:

Veruka (Lenina Zuleika Bologna)	Lorna Duval
Basha (Yeliena Oblonska Nogoodska)	Maggie Turner
Gnasha (Alexandra Stalina Schokolata)	Sonia Pearson
Babushka, an old crone	Anne Johnson
Footrotski (Romanov Beria)	John Turner
Piles, an old servant	Michael Langridge
Captain Sodov (Vladimir Pederastovitch)	Robin Duval
Schoolmaster (Pantograf Ivan Feverovitch)	David Pearson
Stationmaster (Peter Stravinsky Behanovitch Porkin)	Tony Worth
Prompt	Monique Fare
A hand pushing a chamber pot	Beth Crowley

The play directed by Michael Green
Setting by John Stacey

PRODUCTION NOTES

Absolute sincerity is the key-note of this piece. The cast are very anxious about doing a Chekov and they are desperately trying. In fact Mrs Venables, the wife of the group's chairman, is taking the lead part herself, and it is not her fault that she has a speech impediment which turns Veruka's tragedy into farce. Lorna Duval, who played our Veruka, is a speech therapist and used her professional knowledge to play as if suffering from what is technically known as a "lateral 's' ". This means that every time the sufferer says an "s" they make a horrid clucking noise and spray spit everywhere, as Veruka does over Gnasha. If this is difficult, a lisp might be substituted.

Incidentally, the local paper committed a happy solecisim when reporting therapist Lorna's appearance at the Shaftesbury. It had the headline

LORNA THE-
RAPIST STARS
IN WEST END

The girls should make a typically Chekovian trio, Veruka heart-broken and suffering, Gnasha serious and protective and Basha absurdly *ingenue* in white dress and ribbons, always playing with flowers or jumping up and down excitedly. This is the sort of part that is often grabbed by someone too old to play it ("rubbish, of course I don't look 40 on the stage, and anyway I'm only 39 . . .").

Footrotski was played as if the part had been given to a very wooden actor, who stood up every time he spoke and then sat down. He looked permanently puzzled. He marched about stiffly, swinging his left arm with his left leg, and had one squeaky shoe, too (buy a squeaker from a joke shop and tape it under the shoe. They wear out quickly, so get several). Piles is the archetypal stock Russian peasant, a part usually given to some long-serving member of the society who will play Piles exactly the same as he does all old men from Polonius to Desdemona's father.

Our Sodov was portrayed as being acted by a very pompous chap (perhaps Mrs Venables' husband) who obviously revelled in playing such a colourful role, only to have his evening wrecked because his spurs kept getting entangled. The spurs are very important. They must catch the eye of the audience, so they need to be *enormous*. We had to construct our own, from metal. As regards the entangling, this can usually be cheated. As long as they *seem* to be entangled that is enough. Sodov can help by being obviously aware of the menace of his spurs (which probably make him walk as if he had a severe rupture).

The samovar is crucial. We used an oil drum, suitably disguised. Or an old tea-urn would do. The whole tap fitting was attached to a cork so when Piles struggled with the tap he pulled off the whole fitting and the cork came too. It is important that the audience realize Piles is having trouble before the calamity. In the Questors' production we had the handle of the spigot come off first, then the the rest of the fitting. If you use a cork don't have hot tea—it makes the cork swell and one night in Edinburgh it wouldn't come out, a situation which was genuine Course Theatre, and poor Piles wrestled desperately with the samovar. Fortunately, he won. Make sure the samovar is placed prominently. It is important that the audience can see the constant stream of tea all the time. Lots of rehearsal is needed to get the flow correct and for Piles to become an expert in thrusting his various containers under it. An absorbent mat, painted to look like grass or stone, can take any spillage.

The business of passing round the cups as they fill, while ad libbing demands for more tea, must be well-rehearsed. In our production, everyone was left with two cups and the surplus were passed to Babushka, who sat with a pile on her lap (she had a waterproof apron) and eventually teetered out with them. But I saw another production in which Basha finished up with eight, four in each hand.

The ending must be played not only with complete seriousness, but with all the stops out. In fact it would be a tear-jerker but for the fact that Veruka is addressing an empty bench and Piles is dying standing up with his thumb blocking the leak in the samovar. One likes to think what they will all say in the dressing-room afterwards. My guess is that everyone would congratulate Piles on saving the situation. As Sodov would tell him, "Believe me, old man, the audience didn't notice a thing ... Did you notice the clever way in which I covered up that trouble with the spurs ...?"

Acknowledgement

I am deeply grateful to descendants of the late Anton Chekov for not trying to interfere with this production.

MG

THE CHERRY SISTERS

A typical Chekovian exterior. The suggestion of the veranda or garden of a provincial house in Russia. There are several chairs, a bench and a small table, on which stands a samovar. Music plays (probably the theme from "Dr Zhivago")

The three sisters and their brother Footrotski are seated. Basha, the youngest, is playing with a ball made of flowers. Gnasha sometimes sighs. Veruka, the eldest, sits, tragic and sombre. Babushka, an old crone, sits to one side, knitting furiously. There is a long silence. The girls sigh. Footrotski rises and walks a few paces, revealing that his boots creak appallingly and don't fit. He looks at his watch, winds it, sighs and sits down again. Suddenly there is the grinding noise of a tree falling. Babushka cackles. Everyone else jumps

Basha Will we never get to Moscow?

Gnasha One day, Basha, we will get to Moscow.

Veruka (*who has a speech defect*) But how can we get to Moscow, Gnasha? We must stay and look after the estate.

Footrotski (*standing up*) Moscow, Moscow, always Moscow. (*He sits down*)

There is the sound of a tree falling

Gnasha Already they are chopping down the trees to build a railway. How will we live when there are no more trees. We should sell the estate.

Veruka But who would buy an estate with no trees?

Footrotski And a railway running through it?

Gnasha Perhaps Peter Stravinsky Behanovitch Porkin, the Stationmaster, would buy it. He retires next month. Perhaps he would like to spend his twilight days sitting in the living room watching the trains.

Basha (*jumping up and clapping her hands*) Oh, Gnasha! How clever you are! We must ask the Stationmaster to buy the estate. And then we could get to Moscow! How happy I am!

Veruka But how can we get to Moscow? Yesterday Grisha broke his leg and we had to shoot him.

Basha Poor Grisha! I am heartbroken.

Footrotski And then we chopped the troika up for firewood.

Veruka With no pony and no troika, how could we get to Moscow?

There is the sound of a tree falling

Gnasha We could go by train!

Basha (*jumping for joy again*) Oh, Gnasha, how clever you are! When the railway is finished, we can go by train. How happy I am!

Veruka But the line will only go in one direction. East, towards Siberia.

Basha I am heartbroken!

Gnasha Then we must change at Vladivostok.
Basha But how can I go to Moscow with a broken heart?
Veruka Oh, Yeliena Oblonska Nogoodska!
Basha Oh, Lenina Zuleika Bologna!

They embrace. There is the sound of a tree falling

   Piles enters. He is aged 109

Piles The Schoolmaster, Pantograf Ivan Feverovitch, and the Station-master, Peter Stravinsky Behanovitch Porkin, have come to tea.
Veruka They came to tea yesterday.
Basha And the day before.
Gnasha They come every day.
Veruka Nothing changes.
Basha Nothing. Nothing.
Gnasha Nothing.
Footrotski Bring the tea, Piles.
Piles At once, young sir. (*He starts to exit*)
Veruka Piles!

Piles turns in surprise. Veruka makes a series of encouraging grimaces and gestures, then imitates someone riding a horse, clucking her tongue as she does so. Piles watches, fascinated. Suddenly he understands

Piles Oh, yes. Oh, and Captain Sodov is here as well. On his horse.

Veruka swoons rather delicately, making sure she falls gracefully

Basha Alexandra Stalina! The smelling salts!
Piles You ought to burn some rhubarb under her nose. That's what my mother used to do in the old days. We did that when my father had spotted fever.
Gnasha And he recovered?
Piles No, he died.
Footrotski (*standing up*) One feels so useless. If only there was something to be done. We are all doomed. (*He sits down*)

Veruka recovers

Gnasha There, there, my little nightingale.
Basha Perhaps Captain Sodov has come to ask for your hand.
Veruka I don't want to see him! I detest him! Oh, no! Gnasha, I love him! I love him! Do you really think he'll ask me to marry him? Suppose he doesn't. I can't bear it! I don't want to see him! I hate the sight of him!

She showers spit on Gnasha, who flinches. Horse effect is heard, off stage

Gnasha Hush, hush Veruka. He's here.

   Captain Sodov enters in the full uniform of the Imperial Hussars. He walks with difficulty because of his huge spurs

Footrotski Good afternoon, Vladimir Pederastovitch.
Sodov How lovely to see you, Romanov Beria. (*He clicks his heels*)
Veruka How lovely to see you, Vladimir Pederastovitch Sodov.
Sodov Delighted, Lenina Zuleika Bologna.

He turns as he speaks to greet her but his enormous spurs have become entangled and he falls forward clutching at Veruka's skirt, which rips open revealing a suspender-belt and stockings. She retires to one side to repair the damage temporarily

  The Schoolmaster and Porkin, the Stationmaster, enter. Porkin carries a large bag

All three visitors then shake hands with everybody else and call them by their full names so that the stage is a babble of noise for some time

Gnasha And how are you, Peter Stravinsky Behanovitch Porkin?
Porkin How do you do Alexandra Stalina Schokolata? And you, Yeliena Oblonska Nogoodska.
Basha So pleased to see you, Peter Stravinsky Behanovitch Porkin.
Porkin And you, my dear Lenina Zuleika Bologna?

Meanwhile, everyone else is conducting a similar introduction. They then all move round and start again

  Piles enters with a tray of crockery and goes to the samovar

Veruka (*to Porkin*) How is the railway progressing?
Porkin Very well. Yesterday it progressed by six versts. We hope it will reach the station this year.
Gnasha But will it ever get to Moscow?
Porkin In fifty years. Who knows? Perhaps never.
Footrotski At least we can go to Vladivostok in the spring.

Footrotski and Porkin both retire up stage, perfectly together, as if on strings. They take up new positions with mechanical precision. Piles is trying to turn on the tap on the samovar

Basha How futile it all seems!

The Schoolmaster leads Basha down stage

Schoolmaster Will you marry me, Yeliena Oblonska Nogoodska?
Basha No. (*She sobs and goes to sit on the bench*)

The Schoolmaster retires and collides with Gnasha as she crosses to Porkin. She takes Porkin by the arm and drags him to one side

Gnasha Peter Stravinsky Behanovitch Porkin, did Moron Leputkin the Bank Manager, give you any message for me today?
Porkin Yes.
Gnasha What did it say?
Porkin No.

Gnasha weeps. She retires to join Basha sobbing on the bench

Veruka You may serve the tea, Piles.

We now become aware something is wrong with the samovar, with which Piles is struggling. Suddenly the tap fitting comes away

Piles Shit!

A spout of tea comes out. Piles desperately catches it in a cup and when that is full grabs another and passes the full one to whoever is standing nearest. He then repeats the process rapidly. The cups are frantically passed round until everybody has one but still the stream continues. Meanwhile, to cover the crisis, everyone ad libs dialogue as if it were all intentional

All Let me pass you some tea . . . Have another cup of tea . . . This tea is delicious . . . Do have some more . . ., *etc., etc.*

Piles (*as he continues to fill cups*) There is plenty of tea for everyone . . . Here, young sir, do have some more . . . More tea anyone? . . . The tea is still hot . . ., *etc.*

Eventually most people have two cups but they continue to come so they are passed round and finish up with Babushka who gets the lot. Then Piles runs out of cups. As the last one is filling he grabs the hat off the Schoolmaster's head and holds it under the spout

Schoolmaster Well, I'm afraid I must be off.

He tries to take the hat from Piles, who resists. A tug of war, then Piles drags Porkin's bag towards him, opens it to catch the spout and relinquishes the overflowing hat

Good-bye.
All Good-bye, Pantograf Ivan Feverovitch.

The Schoolmaster goes to put on his hat, thinks better of it and exits, carrying his hat carefully

The others gradually unload their crockery, probably on Babushka again

Gnasha We have something very important to ask you, Peter Stravinsky Behanovitch Porkin.
Basha We want you to buy the estate!
Porkin But, dear ladies! Buy the estate? I don't understand.
Veruka Life will not be the same when they have chopped down all our trees and built a railway through the house. It will be unendurable!
Basha But you have lived with trains all your life, Peter Stravinsky. Think how nice it would be to sit in your living room and watch the trains go through.
Porkin But I have no money, only a small pension. How could I afford . . .
Basha Oh, Peter Stravinsky, I'm so unhappy. (*Crying*) Why do they want to build a railway?
Porkin Let me explain, Yeliena Oblonska. I have the plans for the railway in my bag.

He turns to find a stream of tea running into the bag, which is, of course, under the samovar. He tries to take it but Piles blocks him. Piles then notices a small flower basket which Gnasha is holding. He snatches it from her, hurls out the flowers, and substitutes it for Porkin's bag. Porkin takes this and begins his explanation

These plans were produced by the Board to show the proposed route of the railway to Moscow. I'll pass these copies round to each of you.

He pulls some sodden pieces of paper out of the bag and passes them round. All try to look seriously at them, but they keep falling apart

As you can see, the route to Vladivostock runs right through this estate . . . There is no alternative . . . To the north there is the Tamoslit river and to the south the Vrustuk mountains . . . To avoid this area would mean making a loop a hundred miles to the north from Treblinka in the east to Bratislav in the west . . . Already the trees in your orchard are being felled for sleepers . . .

Basha (*covering her ears, crying*) I don't want to hear any more!

She throws away her sodden plan and it hits Porkin

Piles I don't hold with railways. I remember in my father's time when the trains used to stop at the junction to take on board the dead serfs. It was winter, you see, and the ground was too hard to dig graves so we just collected a few every day and drove over to the junction. The rhubarb doesn't grow anymore, not since the great calamity. (*He hastily replaces the almost full basket under the samovar with a vase*)

Gnasha You must not worry, Peter Stravinsky. We will find a way. We will survive.

Porkin Alexandra Stalina, I kiss your hand. (*He does so and also kisses a mass of soggy paper*)

Sodov (*taking Veruka aside*) Lenina Zuleika, I have something to say to you.

Veruka Yes, Vladimir Pederastovitch?

Sodov I have to tell you that my regiment is being posted to Siberia.

Veruka Siberia!

Sodov This is the last time that I shall be able to visit this estate. I must take my leave of you.

Veruka How can I bear to go on living! Will we never see you again?

Sodov Perhaps. When the railway is built you might come to Siberia.

Veruka But Siberia is so far away. And perhaps we will go to Moscow. Who knows?

Sodov So then, we must part. Give me leave to kiss your hand.

Veruka is still holding two cups so he kisses those instead

Goodbye, Lenina Zuleika Bologna.

Veruka goes to reply, but dries

Veruka Goodbye . . . er . . .

Prompt (*off*) Vladimir Pederastovitch . . .
Veruka Goodbye Vladimir Pederastovitch . . .
Prompt (*off*) Sodov.
Veruka Sodov!

Sodov bows. His spurs entangle again. He sways and nearly falls, clinging to Veruka for support. But he recovers and exits hopping on both legs

Porkin I'd better be off too.
Basha I'll see you to the door.
Gnasha We'll all see him off, won't we Veruka?
Veruka Yes, we'll all see him off.
Footrotski Wait for me. I need some more billiard chalk.

All except Piles exit. Babushka does so with difficulty, as she is still holding a lot of cups in her apron. As she disappears into the wings, a crash is heard, off

Piles is left alone on stage with the leaking samovar. He has run out of containers and is stopping the leak with his thumb. But he has to make a dying speech while resting on the garden seat, so he moves to it and leaves the water dribbling into the nearly-full vase

Piles So I'm all alone. They've forgotten about old Piles. I'll just lie down on the bench and rest for a moment . . . My heart's not been too good recently . . . How dark it's getting.

Veruka enters

Veruka Piles!

She rushes to the bench just as Piles realizes the container under the samovar is nearly full, and gets up to plug the leak with his fingers again. Veruka kneels by an empty bench, hesitates and decides to make the best of it

Piles! Are you ill? What's wrong? Why are you staring at me like that? Why are your hands so cold? Why are you trembling?

Piles gives a series of death rattles and tries to die standing by the samovar

Piles! Oh Piles, don't leave us! (*She sobs on the empty bench*)

A chamber pot is pushed in to Piles, who snatches it gratefully and pushes it under the leak. He subsides, as the Lights fade to a Black-out

LAST CALL FOR BREAKFAST

(*Dernier Appel au Petit Déjeuner*)

LAST CALL FOR BREAKFAST

(Dernier Appel au Petit Déjeuner)

By Richard Gaunt and Michael Langridge

First performed at the George Square Theatre, Edinburgh, on August 20th, 1979, and subsequently at the Shaftesbury Theatre, London, with the following cast:

She	Sonia Pearson
He	Richard Gaunt
A Cube of Sugar	Lorna Duval
A Croissant	Michael Green

The play directed by Michael Green
Setting by John Stacey

Scene: A breakfast table near Paris
Time: Eternity

PRODUCTION NOTES

This is a pastiche of Samuel Beckett and others of his school, and the two main characters should echo the staccato Beckett speech rhythms. Both **She** and **He** can act to some extent but their performances are wrecked by a simple mischance, namely that **He** gets into the wrong pot in the black-out. Another over-ambitious production made worse by intellectual pretensions. Perhaps the group's one and only attempt at the *avant-garde* ("I told you we should have done *Bedroom Farce*").

Sugar Cube strikes me as rather different from the other two players. She has obviously been pressurized into the part and is acutely embarrassed by the whole thing (especially by having to dress up as a sugar cube). The cube can be just a painted cardboard box with a hole for the head and the rest of the costume tights and a skull cap.

She could wear leotard and black tights. **He** could wear black tights, black vest or shirt, and black skull cap. Both should have weird make-ups, perhaps dead white face with strange lines painted on, full of symbolism. It is important to emphasize the attempt at being way-out. Plenty of ghastly *musique concrète* should be played before the action.

This piece will not be so readily identifiable as the others to a non-theatrical audience, so it may be necessary to help them. The best way is a programme note stressing the play's *avant-garde* qualities ("This piece is so experimental even the cast do not know how it is going to end. One performance at Cracow University went on for three days . . ."). Plenty of rubbish of this sort should convince even the thickest that this is a burlesque of something experimental. Or an announcement might be made, such as "We had hoped to have the author here tonight but he will not be able to come as he has been arrested at London Airport for importing obscene literature . . ." Doubtless, groups can think up their own variations.

The salt and pepper pots need great care in construction. They need not be round although we used large cardboard tubes from a local factory which were suitably strengthened. But it might be better to construct a square pot. Note the pot belonging to **He** is not used, so it need not be practical as long as it looks satisfactory.

Then there is the problem of how **He** gets into the girl's pot. It is essential to have a complete black-out for this. If light spill from exit signs and so on breaks this, put on very bright lighting just before the black-out for a dazzle effect on the audience. This gives some ten seconds before they can distinguish things in the gloom, time for **He** to make his move. **He** must appear to be going into his own pot, and the black-out must be timed accordingly. Our **He** jumped into the girl's pot through the top, but obviously a small entrance at the back is preferable if it can be arranged.

When **He** first pops up in the wrong pot the audience must grasp what has happened. It is something of a challenge to **He**, who has to convey the disaster simply by his expression (although perhaps a gasp of surprise might be allowed). **He** is determined to go through with the farce no matter what. **She** is less certain and eventually cracks. Afterwards we suspect they have a terrible row, which starts on stage and probably continues on and off for three years.

After seeing many productions of this piece, I have amended the ending slightly for the third printing of this volume. Formerly, the play ended with the lights fading on the quarrel. This proved rather negative so I have added the business of lifting the pot at the end in an effort to escape, together with a few lines of dialogue. I think this makes a more positive ending, with the sudden blackout on the inappropriate line, "I see the sun". If anyone says altering a play after it's been published for five years is Coarse Playwriting, I wouldn't disagree!

LAST CALL FOR BREAKFAST

A dim, bare stage. A noise like somebody testing bedsprings in a cave reveals that avant-garde *music is being played*

Two stage-hands carry on a large salt pot and a similar pepper pot and stand between them with folded arms. Pause. They then look at each other and change the pots round, and resume their positions. They place them parallel to the front of the stage and about six feet apart

He and She enter from different sides. They strike an attitude for a moment and then prance down stage with strange movements which have obviously been carefully rehearsed, because we can see He counting the number of steps with painful concentration. They finish down stage level with the pots, one each side. They turn inwards and cross, so their positions are reversed. The cross is done with the same agonizing deliberation as their previous move. They adopt a stance. The man adopts the wrong stance and corrects himself hastily. The stance is that of someone trying to imitate a tree unsuccessfully. They cross again to their original positions. They adopt another stance, this time like somebody scratching their armpits. While the man remains rigid, the girl breaks her stance and moves to the salt pot, which is nearest to her. The stage-hands lift the pot and the girl enters from underneath. The stage-hands move to the pepper pot. The man prances towards it. Before he reaches it there is a total Black-out. There is the sound of a single loud oath. The stage-hands go through the motions of lifting up the pepper pot in the Black-out and then leave

Voice (*off; on echo*) Dernier appel au petit déjeuner . . . dernier appel au petit déjeuner . . . dernier appel au petit déjeuner . . .

There is the sound of a train whistle which fades away and is replaced by more excruciating music. Suddenly a Spot appears on the salt pot. The Girl's head pops out

She Into the light . . . up . . . out . . . hopelessly before my time . . . lost . . . slap . . . panting . . . screaming . . . breathing . . . breath . . . listen, I am here . . . I have become . . . I have become . . . I have become . . .

The Spot snaps out on the salt pot. A Spot comes up on the other pot. No-one appears. Pause. Then there is a loud grunt and the Light switches back to the salt pot to reveal the Man's head sticking out. He is a tight fit and obviously puzzled at being in the wrong pot. He stares round in bewilderment and then decides to make the best of it

He Into the light . . . this is my time . . . awakening . . . dawn . . . realization . . . I come to my senses and gain understanding . . . I produce sounds . . . I clap . . . (*He tries, but cannot move his arms*) . . . listen . . . (*He ducks down inside, in a muffled voice*) Try to move it over there.

The pot wobbles a little way. The Spot goes out

She It's no use.
He Open your legs!

The Spot comes up uncertainly on the pepper pot and then goes back to the salt pot. She pops up

She I see him . . . as on that first day . . . when I saw his face I knew . . . I reached out and touched your forehead with my hand like this . . .

She goes down. He pops up

He First one up always made tea . . . green tea . . . green.

He goes down. She pops up

She Pea green; sea green; green as gangrene . . . (*She goes down*)

He pops up, dries and goes down again. She is heard prompting him from inside the pot. After a pause He comes up

He Yes, the cat . . . always the cat . . . stretching . . . (*He goes down*)
She Morning and stretching . . . up . . . look up . . . remember how we fructified . . . dark . . . darkness . . . dark.

The Spot on the salt fades

> *Another Spot comes up on Sugar Cube, who suddenly appears down stage. She wears a cardboard box painted like a wrapped cube of French sugar round her shoulders and is clearly embarrassed by the whole thing*

Sugar Cube They saw . . . spoke . . . touched . . . learnt . . . discovered . . . became fulfilled . . . consumed the fruit . . . (*Long pause*) . . . Sweetness, and temptation, tentative exploration, emotional demonstration, mutual acclamation, savage proceation, feeble explanation, guilty accusation . . . (*Pause*) . . . Sudden separation . . . silence . . . separation . . . darkness . . .

The Spot goes out on Sugar Cube and comes up on the pot. The man and woman come up together and are stuck with a terrible gasp

She You are no longer there . . . you have gone completely.

He struggles to get down but can't

> Invisible . . . I no longer see you . . .

There is a further struggle

> Where are you I wonder?
He I'm stuck.
She Are you above me?
He I'm stuck.
She Are you below me?
He I'm stuck.
She This is ridiculous. I can't go on.

He You've got to go on. The audience haven't noticed a thing.

She I've told you, I can't go on. I always said we should have done *Bedroom Farce*.

He Rubbish. Lift the bastard. (*He smiles desperately at the audience*)

With a great heave and a grunt they manage to lift the pot an inch or two and move it slightly before dropping it

He I am rooted to the earth.

He ⎫
She ⎭ (*together*) Ugh!

The "Ugh!" is a joint grunt as they lift the pot after the line and drop it

She I cannot move.

He ⎫
She ⎭ (*together*) Ugh!

Again they grunt and lift and drop the pot

He My roots go down.

He ⎫
She ⎭ (*together*) Ugh!

They lift the pot, move and drop it as before

She But I look up. I see the sun.

This is an unfortunate line as the Stage Manager at last decides to pull the plug and there is a sudden Black-out, followed by male and female cries of distress. The CURTAIN falls, trapping Sugar Cube in front of it. She stares wildly round as the House Lights go up and then tries to force her way through. As she has no free arms or hands she is left kicking and butting at the CURTAIN until a hand reaches out and suddenly pulls her inside. If the piece is done without a curtain she should stand alone and terrified, blinking at the Audience for a moment before sidling off, trying to appear invisible

HENRY THE TENTH (PART SEVEN)

The True Historie and Tragicke Death of
HENRY THE TENTH (PART SEVEN)
Containing an exact representation of the
Coronation of King Henry the Eleventh at
Westminster

By Michael Green
From a suggestion by William Shakespeare

First performed at the George Square Theatre, Edinburgh, on August 20th, 1979, and later at the Shaftesbury Theatre, London, with the following cast:

Clodpony	John Turner
Hayseed	Robin Duval
Chorus	Tony Worth
Drummer	Richard Johnson
King Henry the Tenth	David Pearson
Queen Catherine	Maggie Turner
Old Meg (yet another crone)	Anne Johnson
Lord Uxbridge	Michael Langridge
Lord Amersham	John Turner
Lord Ongar	Richard Gaunt
Herald	Tony Worth
Cuthbert, Earl of Wolverhampton	Robin Duval
Lord Dudley	Richard Lewis and Paul Collins
Baron Smethwick	Richard Gaunt
Clown	Brian Pickles
Messenger	Richard Johnson
Ladies-in-Waiting	Lorna Duval, Sonia Pearson

**Soldiers, Citizens, Priest, and various all-purpose Coarse
parts:** Sonia Pearson, Lorna Duval, Richard Johnson,
Richard Lewis, Brian Pickles, John Stacey, Chris
Lejeune, Paul Collins, Michael Green

A Human Cleat Lesley Montgomery

The play directed by Michael Green
Setting by John Stacey

PRODUCTION NOTES

Like Moby Dick, this piece has a rather over-ambitious director. In writing the script, I have tried to cram in as many Shakespearean clichés as possible, and obviously the play should be directed with an eye to burlesquing the stock ideas of so many Shakespearean productions. Deadly earnestness is the keynote. Our King had plainly based his performance on Laurence Olivier as Henry V while our Earl of Wolverhampton had based his performance on Laurence Olivier as Richard III, although he felt Wolverhampton should have a Birmingham-type accent and duly produced one. Uxbridge plainly considered he was the real lead. Of the other characters, some could act and others were plainly following instructions as in any amateur Shakespeare production. The unfortunate herald was obviously not enjoying his role and we felt he would resign afterwards (". . . as a member for many years I have never been so humiliated on stage . . .").

The important thing, however, is to satirize the stock business from which poor Shakespeare suffers, the artificial stance of the courtiers, with one foot carefully placed forward, the ritual sword fights, the all-purpose Coarse deaths. Our soldiers were particularly striking. They represented every Coarse Shakespeare army ever seen—dressed in obscene cotton tights with holes, knitted chain-mail helmets, and carrying spears that bent, they surged to and fro across the stage with incredible and largely misplaced energy.

Obviously any variations a director can make on the sword fights are welcome as long as they mirror the real thing. One director put a strobe on every fight, which is not so exaggerated as it may seem as I have just seen a production of *Richard III* at the National Theatre where the sound of swords clashing was magnified to an enormous degree. I have also seen Shakespeare productions where sparks flew from the swords. A variant is to use other weapons, such as maces or battle-axes.

But please remember the importance of playing seriously. The play must still hang together as a genuine piece. Then the impact of what goes wrong will be more effective.

As regards the scenery, our designer produced two hollow towers, painted on one side like battlements and on the other side like trees. Operators stood inside these, and they turned round and glided about as required, occasionally forgetting what they had to do and prompting each other by nudging, not to mention colliding with incoming actors. But there is so much scope for satirizing Shakespeare scenery that I have not specified too much detail. Designers may prefer to have their set glide in on castors, or come together in two halves, or be painted on the back of something else, or indeed any of the ways popular in Shakespeare productions. Simple cut-outs or painted flats can also be used. It might be a good idea to have some meaningless rostra around. I saw one very successful production where the scenery merely consisted of two identical cut-outs, representing bushes, which every so often were changed over for a switch of scene.

A technical note: Our Herald's much-abused trumpet was made from thick paper or thin cardboard. This means it is necessary to make a new one for every performance, but paper does bend easily into some lovely shapes. For the King's stretcher, we used hessian attached to two poles with *Velcro*. When carried in, the King supported his weight on the poles by putting his legs over them. When the soldiers came to pick him up, he lay unsupported on the hessian and a sharp pull was enough for the poles to come away.

The doll which represents the infant Prince and which is torn to pieces at the end should present no problem. If necessary, the limbs and the head can be separated beforehand and refixed so as to come off easily.

This script is based on the original production in which the army was filled out with dummies, owing to a shortage of actors. There is no need for this if there are enough men to go round. Even if not, a tiny army might be more typical of Course Acting and hence funnier than the use of dummies. It is tempting to fill up the army with women but in my experience this rarely works. It is too far from reality. The more realistic the army, the funnier they will be. And that goes for everything else about the production, too.

ACT I

SCENE 1

Westminster. A funeral bell is tolling. Solemn music and drums. If there are enough spare players, people may totter about the stage indicating deep grief

Hayseed and Clodpony enter. Clodpony is enveloped in cloak and hood and is bent double with a stick for support. This is partly because he is doubling something else and doesn't want to be recognized. Hayseed is covered in straw because he is called Hayseed. Their performances are totally standard characterizations, that is to say they speak like mangel-wurzles and move about all the time illustrating each word with gestures

Hayseed Why, 'tis Master Clodpony!

Clodpony Good cheer, Master Hayseed!

Hayseed What means the bell, good neighbour Clodpony?

Clodpony Why, know you not Master Hayseed? (*As the next few lines are plot-stuff he turns to face the audience and says them very carefully*) 'Tis for the King, he that was Henry the Ninth and who is dead, and whose coffin shall pass this way quickly.

Hayseed Then he yet lives, for if his coffin pass quickly, he is alive, being yet quick.

He emphasizes the joke heavily, as the Director has told him this is funny, and probably beats Clodpony on the back. Clodpony goes into an exaggerated paroxysm of mirth, beating his stick on the ground and finally hitting his toe. He gives a cry of pain

Clodpony Nay, he is dead, birlady and God's sonties, as dead as a Black-friars bull at Michaelmas. (*Once more he turns to the audience*) I fear for his brother good Henry the Tenth who succeeds him. For the barons wish evil toward him and I fear he will have a sorry reign.

Hayseed By the rood thou'rt melancholy. An' were I king I would be as merry as a flea in a midwife's ear.

Clodpony I would thou wert a midwife's ear, good Master Hayseed, then thou might listen to me betimes. But soft, the funeral procession comes.

They retire. Both go the wrong way and collide, and then sort themselves out and exit, Clodpony limping

The funeral procession enters, headed by a Priest waving a thurible which fills the stage with choking smoke. He is followed by a procession of Lords, Nobles, Ladies-in-Waiting, etc., headed by the new King and Queen with Old Meg, Soldiers and anybody who can be spared. The procession moves a pace at a time, perfectly in step. Halfway through it is the coffin, carried by Soldiers. As the front of the procession gets near the wings, everyone speeds up and rushes off, to re-appear at the back of the pro-cession. This should go on until at least three or four have reappeared on stage at the back of the procession. At this point there is a hiatus as they can't get the coffin into the wings. The Soldiers struggle for a moment and then turn round and start to march off the other way. After some confusion, the procession reverses itself, and returns, trying, unsuccessfully, to keep its dignity, as the return journey becomes a panic-stricken rout, with the coffin at the rear. There is further difficulty getting the coffin into the wings

The Lights fade to a Black-out

SCENE 2

A tucket. Drums. The Chorus enters, followed by a Drummer who makes occasional rolls. Behind him two Soldiers are still struggling to get the coffin off, which they eventually do by standing it on end

Chorus (*who obviously fancies himself as a speaker*)
    Now England mourns the death of Henry Nine,
    Noblest of monarchs all, who capturéd
    Fair Edinburgh from off the gallant Scot
    And worthiest grandson of Henry Eight.
    So now in London reigns his brother Henry,
    Tenth in that noble line of mighty kings.
    But picture a state divided;
    All England lies and bleeding torn asunder.
    For in the dark and gurdy north now see
    How vile rebellion rears its ugly head
    And Cuthbert, Earl of Wolverhampton
    Claiming the throne is his by right of birth . . .

At this point he is interrupted by the Drummer who marches around madly drumming. The next lines are completely drowned

    Has raised his standard 'gainst the lawful Crown
    And gathered round his all-rebellious flag . . .

This cannot be heard. The Chorus glares. The Drummer subsides

    A group of scheming disappointed men
    Who for the sake of paltry gain will sell
    Their everlasting souls and risk the flames
    Of hell itself to gain a little land . . .

The Drummer approaches loudly and menacingly and the Chorus moves, his voice rising to a crescendo

    Evesham and Tewkesbury, I will name them all,
    Dudley and Smethwick, companions in their crimes
    And worst of all, vile Wolverhampton.
    So now the scene is set. To London make
    Where Henry and his Lords do counsel take.

The Drummer ceases abruptly just before the last few words which come out as a husky bellow. The Chorus exits, clutching his throat. The Drummer follows

Black-out

SCENE 3

The palace in London. The Lights come up on the Lords Uxbridge, Amersham and Ongar grouped around an empty area in the centre of the stage

The King is pushed in on his throne, mounted on a stage truck. This should have been done in the Black-out but the King was late. He shoots past the Lords through the specially-lighted area and grinds to a halt down stage. He stares around wildly. The Lords kneel. Rise. Kneel. Rise

King Arise good gentles all.

The Lords kneel

Come brave Uxbridge, Ongar, Amersham, what is the news from Wolverhampton?

The Lords don't know what to do. The King impatiently waves them to come down stage. They move down and group around him. During the next few speeches, the lighting builds up to an overall brightness

Uxbridge Even at this moment, My Liege, we expect a herald from the rebel lords at Dudley Castle.

Thinking to move the King back, he puts his foot on the truck which promptly swings round, turning the King up stage and revealing "Wanted for Henry X" chalked on the back of the throne

King It likes us not. (*He realizes he is speaking up stage while his Lords are down stage and twists round to speak over the back of his throne*) It likes us not. For when rebellion raises its evil standard in the land
'Tis like unto a serpent in the nest
An adder on the hearth, a rat at night
Or like some filthy, loathsome plague
Which must be scotched ere the state is whole.

Ongar, in another attempt to help, pushes the front of the truck with his foot, leaving the King speaking with his face twisted over the back of the throne. He twists front again

So, let our royal pronouncement be this task
No mercy till they do for pardon ask!

Amersham But see, where comes a herald apace, My Liege. Perchance he is from Wolverhampton.

A Herald enters. He raises his long trumpet to his mouth. Silence. Suddenly there is a blast of sound beginning with a sort of Y-o-o-p. A fanfare sounds

King Come, speak what thou hast to speak, and that you speak it, pray you speak it hastily. I like not thy looks for I fear thou bring'st bad news from Wolverhampton.

Herald My Liege, I bring a fair offer of peace from my Lord Cuthbert of Wolverhampton and those about him, Dudley, Tewkesbury and the mighty Smethwick.

All react to the names in hostile fashion

King Give us thy fair offer, churl.

Herald That you immediately surrender your throne, unlawfully held from that usurper Henry Nine, Elizabeth's vile bastard, unto my Lord Cuthbert of Wolverhampton, the rightful heir to England as well as thou know'st.

The Lords react to this by repeating key words such as "bastard" angrily. The King rises and seizes the Herald, whom he throws violently to the ground in a cloud of dust

Herald (*sotto voce*) Christ.

King (*kicking him*)
    Thou naughty messenger! Were I as cruel
    As is thy master wanton I would have
    Thee hanged high before the day is out.

As he speaks, he attacks the unfortunate Herald unmercifully. The Lords join in, all kicking and beating the prostrate Herald

    But go to evil Wolverhampton
    And tell him thus: Unless he gives himself
    Into my hands tonight and duly makes
    Submission of the utmost fealty
    I shall not rest until his rebel crew
    Are carrion in the highest gallows tree.
    Go tell him this.

Herald (*rising painfully*) I will, My Liege.

He places his trumpet to his lips but it was broken in the fight and now droops down at right angles. There is, however, a perfect fanfare. He exits

Uxbridge My Liege . . .

There is a brief blast of trumpet which stops abruptly with a screech . . .

    My Liege, this was well done.

King (*broken*) *Et tu*, Wolverhampton?

Amersham Courage, My Lord. Thou wilt see the difference betwixt traitors' hearts and those of loyal men.

Ongar Dread sovereign Liege, if offering my right arm would aid thy cause thou should have it, aye, blood, bones and all. (*He kneels and bares his right arm revealing a wrist-watch. He hurriedly bares the other one*)

King (*moved*) Why that's my valiant Amersham. (*He places his hand on Ongar's shoulder, realizes his error and repeats the line, this time to the correct person*) Thanks, lovely Ongar, and thrice-puissant Uxbridge. There's some loyal yet. (*He totters*) And yet my heart doth nearly break when it ponders upon vile Wolverhampton. Oh revolted Wolverhampton! Oh most hideous Wolverhampton! Ungrateful, base Wolverhampton. (*He totters brokenly to his throne and sits heavily on it. It collapses, trapping him in the wreckage*)

Ongar (*whispering*) Are you all right?

Uxbridge (*brushing him aside*) My Liege . . . you must prepare for battle against vile Cuthbert and the rest.

King (*speaking from a semi-recumbent posture as he struggles unsuccessfully to rise*) Aye, noble lords, to battle then we must
    And fight until rebellion's ugly head
    Is banished from this fair and noble land.
    Go Uxbridge, Amersham and Ongar too,
    Get thee ten thousand men apiece and meet
    Me here tomorrow. See it done.
    No peace in England till the battle's won! (*His voice rises to a shriek but the effect is spoiled as he is partly horizontal*)

All No peace in England till the battle's won!

King (*in pain*) Oh God!

Stage-hands rush to help the King. The throne is suddenly jerked back with the King still in it

All (*dubiously*) No peace in England, till the battle's won!

Exeunt, hesitantly

The Lights fade to a Black-out

SCENE 4

The castle at Dudley. Martial music is playing

The Lights come up on Wolverhampton and Dudley, taking them by surprise, as Dudley is adjusting the hump on Wolverhampton's back. They jerk into character

Dudley And the King, My Lord, has not replied to your fair offer?

Wolverhampton (*in a Birmingham accent*) I expect a herald with his message within the hour.

Dudley Vile usurper! How dare he claim the throne? Thou art the rightful heir, being Elizabeth's son by her secret marriage to Lord Essex.

Wolverhampton The church denies the marriage. Were it not so, all England would be mine. But we shall make it so, brother Dudley.

He is interrupted by a piece of scenery falling down to reveal a stage-hand glued to the back of it. The stage-hand exits

Smethwick, who is doubling Ongar, slinks on, late

Dudley Would that we knew the King's mind.

Smethwick Good news is often a long time coming. Ill news comes soon enow.

Wolverhampton Why that's my brother Smethwick. But hark, methinks I hear a noise without doth signify the arrival of a herald.

The Herald enters. He has left his trumpet in the wings for repair

Come, scurvy messenger. Thy looks I like not. Tell what tidings thou has received from the King.

Herald My Lord . . .

He is interrupted as the trumpet sound comes in perfectly on cue. But he has no trumpet. He registers extreme indecision and embarrassment

My Lord . . . the King rejects outright thy demands and further demands himself that you, together with the good Lords Dudley and Smethwick surrender yourselves to his good mercy. Otherwise from the highest gallows thou shalt hang. Thus said the King.

Wolverhampton Say'st thou so?

He picks up the long-suffering Herald by the clothes and hurls him to the ground

Then that's for thee, filthy bearer of ill-tidings. I'll teach thee talk of hanging to us here! From my sight get thee hence.

Once more all three beat up the Herald

Herald (*in pain*) I will, My Lord.

The Herald exits

Dudley What now, My Lord Cuthbert?

Wolverhampton Why war of course! Bloody, savage, pitiless war! We will lay waste the kingdom until the King accepts our just demands.

He wildly criss-crosses the stage as he says this speech. The others try to keep up

Smethwick The King shall know the mettle of our minds.

Dudley And perchance the metal of our swords.

Wolverhampton That were a hot answer.

Smethwick Aye, as hot as blood.

Wolverhampton Then 'twere good, being hot-blooded.

Dudley But we shall cool the King's blood.

Smethwick King's blood, say'st thou? Nay, we shall cool the bones and all ere we are finished!

This exchange ends in a mutual paroxysm of mirth. The others slap Smethwick on the back. A cloud of dust arises

Wolverhampton Why that's my witty Smethwick. Thou wert ever ready with a merry quip. But 'tis no time to jest and dally now. Let's meet tomorrow armed to meet the foe. But first, we swear on our swords. Swear!

Wolverhampton and Dudley draw swords and cross them. Smethwick tries to draw his but it is jammed in the scabbard. He gives up and holds up his arm as a sword and they all cross

Death to the tyrant Henry the Tenth! Swear!
All Death to the tyrant Henry the Tenth!

They stand awkwardly in pose waiting for a Black-out which does not come. The cast for the next scene can be seen hovering in the wings

SCENE 5

The palace at Westminster

The King, Queen, Clown, Old Meg (a nurse) with infant prince (a doll), Ladies-in-waiting etc. enter

Wolverhampton, Dudley and Smethwick sheepishly exit

The others dance a gavotte which starts well but ends in disaster. Another of Mrs Venables' failures

Clown (*singing*)
Why does my lover fly away?
Dildo, dildo, fiddle-diddle-dildo.
And why do women weep perdy?
Dildo, dildo, fiddle-diddle-dildo.
For men must go and women weep
Dildo, dildo, fiddle-diddle-dildo.
And all a-long life's but a cheat
Dildo, dildo, fiddle-diddle-dildo.

Unless a castrated actor can be found, the Clown can mime to someone singing in impossibly high pitch on tape. During the song he goes around beating people over the head with a bladder

Queen And thou must indeed go to fight these rebels, My Lord?
King Aye, I must.
Queen Can no tongue persuade you from this bloody course?
King No, none that woman hath.
Queen Yet think of thy infant son, perhaps left fatherless while he yet toothless hangs upon the dug. (*She indicates the doll in Old Meg's arms*)

Sound effect of baby crying. The King moves to Meg and tries to take the baby

King My infant son, the future King of England! (*He goes to take the baby but its shawl has caught in one of Meg's buttons and after a brief struggle he abandons the attempt*)

Old Meg Peace, little one. Alas, I fear thou shalt have crying enow, ere
long.

Clown Nuncle, good nuncle, answer me this riddle.

King To't poor fool.

Clown Why is a candlestick-maker like a codpiece?

All register extreme amusement because the Director has told them to

King Nay, I know not, unless it be that both hold that which is dear. (*He
clutches his loins to emphasize the jest*)

Everyone laughs hollowly again

Clown Thou makest light of the jest, nuncle. Ergo, thou art a candlestick-
maker, for he maketh light all the time.

King But I am no codpiece, thou rogue.

Clown Nay, for a codpiece comes down betimes.

The ladies look suitably shocked

    And thou wilt never bend nuncle.

King (*laughing artificially*) There's wisdom in thy madness, fool.

Clown Aye, nuncle, I can tell a fart by moonlight.

*An exaggerated explosion of mirth by all and Old Meg, whose mirth turns to
genuine choking. She flings the doll aside roughly as she doubles up coughing,
attended by the other women. But the coughing won't subside and she teeters
into the wings, where she can be heard calling for water and gasping*

King No more, prithee good fool, lest I die from the sharpness of thy wit.

A Messenger enters

Messenger My Liege, the rebel host with fifty thousand men is marching
upon St Albans.

*He goes out the wrong side, and tip-toes back across the stage, interrupting
the King*

King 'Tis meet we go and that we go 'tis meet.
        Ourselves must arm against the foe at once.
        War's dogs will not wait, even for the King.
        And so I bid farewell to my brave Kate,
        If not on earth, we meet at Heaven's gate!
        Let's kiss my babe once more.

*He looks round for the babe, and discovers it on the floor. He picks it up
and kisses it with some distaste, and then still carrying it, kisses the Queen.*

He exits absentmindedly carrying the child by one foot

Queen Farewell, brave Henry, I fear I shall never see thee more. I kiss thy
infant son instead of thee . (*She cannot*)

Old Meg returns, somewhat husky, and starts looking for the doll

Old Meg Bear up madam, perdy thou shalt see the King again ere long.
Queen Never Meg, never, never, never.
Old Meg Alack the day!
All Oh woe, alack the day.
Queen (*after a vain search*) Sweet infant baby, thou art all I have.

*The King returns hastily and roughly thrusts the doll at the nearest person.
He exits again*

*A Lady-in-waiting tip-toes to the Queen with the doll but she doesn't notice.
The Lady-in-waiting draws her attention by tapping her on the shoulder with
the doll. The Queen interrupts her speech and takes it*

All England's hopes must now flow in thy veins.
Thy father goes to battle in the morn.
Alack the dreadful day that thou was born!
Old Meg Oh woe! Alack the day.
All Oh woe! Alack the day.

The Lights fade to a Black-out, as grim music plays

ACT II

The Chorus enters. The Drummer can be heard drumming off stage

Chorus
> Now all of England madly is on fire
> Cuthbert of Wolverhampton, with the Lords
> Of Smethwick, Dudley and of Evesham
> March north and south and east and west
> Spreading destruction.
> Alas, poor Henry, his kingdom torn by strife
> An army scarce can raise. So for a while . . . (*He tails off*)

The mad Drummer appears as before, obliterating the Chorus

The Chorus raises his voice and retreats

> An army scarce can raise. So for a while
> The rebels have their way, on London march,
> And ugly rebellion for a spell is king
> Until the King's own power is musteréd.
> Which when it is, then battle joinéd is.

He exits, followed by the Drummer

Black-out

SCENE 2

A wood near St Albans. Trees are set. Bird noises

The rebel Lords—Wolverhampton, Dudley and Smethwick—enter, armed

Wolverhampton Here will we halt awhile, and perchance hear tidings of the King.
Dudley What call they this place?
Wolverhampton St Albans, brother Dudley. But soft, who is this approaches through the trees?
Smethwick 'Tis a herald. Berlike he comes from the King.

Wolverhampton starts his usual maniacal criss-crossing followed by the others

Wolverhampton
> Berlike he doth; and that he doth, berlike.
> I hope the weak and vacillating King
> Is not to offer peace. For now the crown

Of all the kingdom lies within our grasp
And I will have it!
All The crown of England!

*The Herald appears. His trumpet has been repaired and the join concealed
with a handkerchief wrapped round*

*Everyone looks warily as he raises the trumpet to his lips, but the sound is
perfect. Unfortunately, just as they are sighing with relief, at the end there is
a snatch of "Hi-ho, hi-ho" music from "Snow White"*

Herald Dread Lord, I bring tidings from King Henry. He bids me say he
will yet offer fair peace if you will submit yourselves to his good mercy.
Wolverhampton Mercy, quotha! Ha, that's good.
All Ha, ha, ha.
Wolverhampton Go, thou wartish dungheap, and carry our defiance to the
King.

*He seizes the unfortunate Herald, throws him down and subjects him to the
now-familiar beating-up, in which the Lords join, kicking in unison*

Tell him that we shall not swerve from our fell purpose until he lays his
life, his throne, his crown at our mercy! Go tell him this.

The Herald arises with his trumpet terribly bent. He looks at it savagely

Herald I will My Lord.

He exits, limping

Dudley What now, My Lord?
Wolverhampton
No rest until the battle's lost and won!
Cry "Esperance Cuthbert" and set on!
All Esperance Cuthbert! And set on!

Exeunt, waving swords

SCENE 3

*Another wood near St Albans. The change is signified by swapping over
identical trees. A tiny rostrum is set for the King*

*The King enters, followed by the Lords Uxbridge, Amersham and Ongar, and
the army. To increase their numbers, some of the Soldiers carry dummy
soldiers between them, whose arms and hands they manipulate*

King (*resting his foot on the rostrum*) What call they this place, good
brother Uxbridge?
Uxbridge It is called St Albans, My Liege.
Amersham The army is so exhausted with marching it can scarcely hold
the pace, My Lord.

The army groans loudly

King Then here we rest. Our army is but a scarecrow, besmirched and bedraggled. See how our men, with weary limbs and bones, lie upon the grass's muddy verge, scorning the moisture of the dew in weariness.

The army lies down with much grunting

Uxbridge My Liege, the herald you sent to the rebel camp has returned.

> *The Herald enters, with his customary air of apprehension. He places his now much-shortened trumpet to his lips. A fanfare sounds*

King Say on speedily what news thou bringest, for I mislike thy complexion and fear thou bringst ill-tidings.

Herald The Lord Cuthbert of Wolverhampton bids me say he scorns your offer of mercy and offers nothing but defiance. Furthermore, he bids me to say he lies but two arrow shots from your camp and will give battle within the hour. (*He cringes, but the King is in a generous mood*)

King To that, no answer's needed but the sword. Here's money for thy pains. (*He snatches a huge and heavy purse of coins from his belt and throws it at the Herald*)

> *The purse catches the Herald in the stomach. He exits, dazed*

Uxbridge Must we fight now, My Liege? My sword is yours but I fear the army's almost spent. (*He offers his sword-hilt to the King*)

King Aye, that we must and speedily.

He brushes away the proffered sword causing the point to strike Uxbridge in the groin, to his great distress

> I'll not believe the soldiers are not ready. Come, good Lord Uxbridge, how are thy privates?

Uxbridge (*with difficulty*) Forsooth, My Liege, they are in good heart. And the officers too.

King For those brave words I love thee, gallant Uxbridge.

He slaps him on the back causing further pain. Uxbridge's sword, which was resting by his foot, goes through the foot of his armour and pins him to the stage. The King jumps on to the little rostrum which was set earlier for this purpose. A Spot comes up on him

> Now let us fall upon the rebel host!
> And he that is too tired to fight depart
> He shall be free to go, I promise him.

The Soldiers rise and group round him, repeating the last words of every line in the manner of all Coarse crowds, and supporting the dummies between them. They manipulate the dummies, waving their arms and talking to them

> Who'd sleep when so much glory's to be won?

All Glory, sleep, glory . . ., *etc.*

King If fate should choose we are to die today . . .

All Die, fate . . ., *etc.*
King Let's die at least with armour on our backs!
All Yes, armour, backs, backs.
King

>Dudley, Smethwick and Wolverhampton vile
>Ravish and threaten all throughout the land.

All Land, land.
King

>They covet not the crown alone, good friends
>But you, your very cattle and your wives.

All Wives, wives.

This degenerates into a paroxysm of reaction and the crowd get out of hand, waving the dummies' arms wildly and shouting. The King cannot continue, until he steps forward and silences them with a glare

King The little infant prince would not be spared.

All groan

>Naught would be sacred to that evil band.

All Evil band, evil band.
King So let us pledge ourselves and raise our arms . . .
All Arms, arms.
King On to St Albans! Henry and St George!
All On to St Albans! Henry and St George!

>*They rush off in a mad surge of patriotic fervour, trampling all over the King who is knocked down. He gets up with his crown askew. At this moment the back of the whale from Moby Dick tentatively appears on stage and withdraws quickly. The King looks at it in surprise and then begins to teeter off*

King (*feebly*) On to St Albans, Henry and St George!

>*He exits, as the Lights fade to a Black-out*

SCENE 4

Part of the battle. Alarums, excursions and battle noises

Two Soldiers carrying spears rush across the stage, shouting madly, and go off the other side. There is a pause, and then the same two rush madly back across the stage again

A Soldier runs in carrying a dummy on the end of his spear and shouting aggressively at it. He exits

Another Soldier comes on, fiddling with a trick arrow. He eventually gets it to work so it appears to stick in his chest. Blood spouts all over the place as he chews a capsule. He dies and crawls off

Two Soldiers come on fighting, by crossing spears and grunting and forcing each other back and forward. One falls and is despatched under the armpit. The victor walks off, the body crawls off

The battle noises stop abruptly

Smethwick and Amersham enter in tatty chain-mail, carrying swords and shields

Amersham Stay, rebellious Smethwick.
Smethwick Stay, treacherous Amersham.
Amersham Stay, say's thou? Then stay upon thy stay or I'll unstay thee!

They clash shields. Suddenly Amersham drops dead for no apparent reason. Smethwick looks embarrassed and taps him with his sword. He raises his head

Smethwick (*in a whisper*) No, you kill me. (*He points to his armpit*)

Amersham realizes his mistake and rises

Amersham Then die, filthy Smethwick! (*He makes a formal pass in Smethwick's direction*)

Smethwick Oh, I am slain. (*He dies*)
Amersham So perish all traitors.

Amersham exits

Uxbridge and Wolverhampton enter from opposite sides. Wolverhampton is dressed in chain-mail armour two feet too long, which looks as if it might come down at any moment. Both carry enormous two-handed swords which are much too heavy for them

Uxbridge Wolverhampton!
Wolverhampton Uxbridge!
Uxbridge Of all traitors the most base and vile. How have I sought thee in battle! (*He raises his huge sword high and lets it fall heavily*)
Wolverhampton And I thee, perfidious Uxbridge. (*He whirls his mighty sword round his head and loses control*)
Uxbridge Then lay on Cuthbert, for one of us shall never see tomorrow's dawn. (*Once more he raises his sword high above his head and this time he overbalances backwards. The sword sticks in the floor and he is left horizontal, with knees bent, still clutching it*)
Wolverhampton Let it be thee, fawning Uxbridge.

He whirls his sword and this time the momentum carries him past the recumbent Uxbridge and off stage, where a banging and crashing suggests he is having trouble

Uxbridge rises and looks off after him

Wolverhampton suddenly appears at the other side of the stage. Uxbridge doesn't notice, so Wolverhampton coughs to draw his attention

Uxbridge turns and they fight. Owing to the weight of the swords it is difficult. Their first parry sees them both out of control and colliding helplessly so they have to hold on to each other. They recover and manage two magnificent parries but the weight of the swords tells and the parries get lower and lower until they are merely scratching the ground each time. They recover and lock swords, trampling to and fro over the recumbent Smethwick, who complains bitterly and crawls to a safer position. Eventually Wolverhampton raises his sword for a mighty blow and it flies backwards out of his hands. He drops exhausted. Uxbridge, who can hardly stand with exhaustion, makes a feeble pass on the floor near him and Wolverhampton dies

Uxbridge Then farewell traitor, thy end was as ignoble as thy life.

The King enters with the Lords Amersham and Uxbridge. The remains of the army—two Soldiers—escort the prisoner Dudley, who is bound with a rope

King The rebels flee . . . (*He trips over Smethwick*) The rebels flee the field. The day is ours.
Amersham My Lord, here lies the traitor Wolverhampton.
King Vile Wolverhampton dead! Then is my happiness complete. And Smethwick too I see. Go take up the bodies.

The two Soldiers look at each other. One of them leaves Dudley and goes to pull Wolverhampton off by his feet. Wolverhampton's chain-mail, however, comes away in his hands, revealing that he is wearing rather flashy underwear. The Soldier hurriedly exits with the chain-mail, and Wolverhampton exits in the other direction. The other Soldier tries to drag Smethwick off, who protests, eventually walking off, with the Soldier following

Uxbridge Lord Dudley is taken, My Liege.
King Convey him hence to present execution.

There is no-one to do this. Lord Dudley looks interrogatively at Amersham and Uxbridge but receives a shake of the head

Convey him hence to present execution!

Uxbridge motions with his head

Dudley drags himself off by holding the rope in front of him

The King totters

King But all my brain seems in a giddy whirl.
Support me now brave Uxbridge lest I fall.
I am not well. The fevered morning air
Doth seem t' infect my very personage.
Oh ill-starred victory, to save a crown
Must I the rest of my all life lay down?

The Lights fade to a Black-out as music plays: "I vow to thee my country" ("Jupiter" from "The Planet Suite" by Holst)

SCENE 5

The road from St Albans to London

The King is carried in on a stretcher by two Soldiers and accompanied by his Lords Uxbridge, Amersham and Ongar

King Set me down here awhile. The heavy hand of death is on my nostrils.

The Soldiers drop him heavily

Oh God, my back again!

Uxbridge Oh cursed spite!

Amersham Oh perfidious fortune that the King should be dying in his hour of triumph from a fever on the battle field.

All Oh woe.

King Uxbridge, good Ongar, Amersham. Come closer to me now, I have but scant accomodation left upon this globe.

Uxbridge (*sobbing*) Oh hideous fate! These tears unman me!

He sobs upon the King, masking him. The King swiftly moves Uxbridge's head to one side

King (*panting*) Now straight I charge ye this upon your souls:
    My infant son, who yet doth suck the breast
    See crowned Henry, Eleventh in the line,
    At Westminster. Go see this done and I
    Shall pray for you forever. (*He wheezes heavily as if suddenly attacked by asthma, to show he is dying*)

Uxbridge It shall be done, My Liege.

King Then I shall quit this earth with happy dole. But first there's one more thing to say on this. Uxbridge come closer, for 'tis growing dark . . . (*He gurgles and dies at some length, carefully arranging himself on the stretcher*)

Uxbridge He's dead. (*This is the understatement of the year*) England's dead. Hope's dead. All's dead.

Amersham Mine eyes will burst with sobbing.

Ongar Would that tongue could tell of my grief.

All Woe, woe.

Uxbridge Come take up noble Henry and carry him to Westminster, there to see the infant Henry the Eleventh crowned King of England in his stead.

The Soldiers take up the stretcher, but the poles come away, leaving the King on the ground. After a moment's confusion he gets up and walks off inside the two poles with the Soldiers carrying them. The Lords follow them off, as sad music plays and the Lights fade to a Black-out

SCENE 6

Westminster. The Coronation

*A procession enters—Uxbridge and the other Lords, the Queen, Archbishop,
Herald, Soldiers etc. Old Meg carries the infant*

All God save the King! God save the King!
Uxbridge Come, good Meg, give me the infant and let me show him to the
people. 'Tis meet they see their new-crowned sovereign Liege.
Meg With all my heart, sweet Lord. Good babe, leave my dug and go to
the noble Lord.

Uxbridge takes the doll

Queen Let the people see this fatherless infant, the King of England!
Uxbridge Herald, go sound a blast of exultation to our King.

*The long-suffering Herald steps forth and raises his trumpet, still carrying the
emergency bandage. The sound of a thunderstorm comes forth*

Uxbridge Do ye wish to see your King?
All Aye, aye. The King! The King!
Uxbridge Then according to our custom I shall present him thrice.
Behold your dread sovereign, Henry the Eleventh.

*He goes to hold up the doll but drops it. Ongar, trying to pick it up, steps
forward and grabs the head. Uxbridge savagely tries to tear the doll from
Ongar's grasp and the head and a leg come off. He stuffs the leg into the neck*

(*Holding up the mutilated doll*) Behold your dread sovereign Henry the
Eleventh.
All God save the King.

*He repeats this twice more, the crowd's answer growing more dubious each
time, and then throws the headless doll savagely to the Queen*

Uxbridge Then that's well done and England has a King. God save the
King! And bear him hence in triumph.

Queen Sweet infant Henry, now I kiss thy face
        In token of the love all England bears.

*She looks dubiously at the mutilated doll. Ongar hands her the head. She kisses
it and returns it to him. Then she leads the procession off stage, cradling the
doll*

All *(As they exit)* Long life to Henry the Eleventh! Long life to Henry the
Eleventh!

All except Uxbridge exit

The Lights dim to a Spot on Uxbridge

Uxbridge As for ourselves we have no rest this day.

The spot tries to contract and he tries to get his face into it

For news comes from the North that even now
The weasel Scot is armed and on the march.

He goes on his knees in an effort to keep up with the diminishing Spot

This hapless babe inherits bloody strife
Yet England still has hope while he has life.

By now he is lying on the floor, trying to get his face into a Spot about one foot wide. It blacks out on him

Note: The above ending is as performed in the original production. But the ending is perfectly effective without a spotlight or any tricks. Uxbridge's voice should rise to a triumphant bellow and be followed by lots of brave music. In some earlier versions I added an alternative finish for those without a spotlight. This is now omitted. On reflection I felt it was an invitation to a genuine Coarse disaster, with somebody working from a different script to everyone else ...

MOBY DICK
FURNITURE AND PROPERTY LIST

On stage: Inn-sign for the *Try Pots Inn*

Off stage: Sea-bag **(Ishmael)**
Trestle table **(Seamen)**
Benches **(Seamen)**
Cardboard beer mugs **(Serving Wenches)**
Fake concertina **(Seaman)**
Harpoon on rope **(Queequeg)**
Shoe (to go on harpoon) **(Stage management)**
Pulpit with rope ladder **(Congregation)**
Bollards with ropes **(Seamen)**
Cut-out of the *Pequod* **(Seamen)**
Deck-rail **(Seamen)**
Capstans **(Seamen)**
Ropes **(Seamen)**
Grog bottle **(Seaman)**
Hammer **(Carpenter)**
Cut-out of the *Rachel* **(Stage management)** *Optional*
Dummy **(Stage management)**
Cup of water **(Stage management)**
Whaling boat **(Seamen)**
Harpoon **(Ahab)**
Smaller cut-out of the *Pequod* **(Stage management)**
Harpoon **(Ahab)**
Whale **(Spare actors)** *See Production Notes on p. 6*

Personal: **Seamen:** eye-patches
Ahab: crutch
Ahab: gold coin

LIGHTING PLOT

Property fittings required: nil
Various exterior and interior settings

To open: House Lights up; warmers on stage; spot on inn-sign

Cue 1	As National Anthem ends *Fade House Lights*	(Page 7)
Cue 2	As music reaches climax *Snap out warmers; snap on follow-spot, wander over stage,* *then snap out. Return to opening lighting, then repeat* *Cue 1*	(Page 7)

Cue 3	**Ishmael** stands shifting his feet *Bring up Spot, just missing* **Ishmael**	(Page 7)
Cue 4	**Ishmael** exits *Fade Spot; bring up Spot on inn-sign and general lighting for inn scene*	(Page 7)
Cue 5	**Seamen** exit *Dim all lighting; bring up Spot, again just missing* **Ishmael**	(Page 10)
Cue 6	**Ishmael** moves across stage *Spot tries to follow him*	(Page 10)
Cue 7	**Ishmael**: ". . . to deliver his sermon . . ." *Fade Spot on* **Ishmael** *and bring up general lighting to previous level*	(Page 10)
Cue 8	As congregation finish singing first verse of hymn *Snap on Spot on pulpit*	(Page 10)
Cue 9	**Queequeg** and **Ishmael** exit *Fade all lighting, pause, then bring up bright lighting for Quay scene*	(Page 10)
Cue 10	The *Pequod* "sails" *Fade to Black-out*	(Page 12)
Cue 11	**Ishmael** enters *Bring up Spot, missing* **Ishmael**; *try to follow him around stage*	(Page 12)
Cue 12	**Ismael**: ". . . a lively set of lads." *Fade Spot on* **Ishmael**; *bring up general lighting for deck scene*	(Page 12)
Cue 13	**Starbuck**: "But not the last." *Dim general lighting; bring up Spot, almost on* **Ishmael**	(Page 15)
Cue 14	**Ishmael**: ". . . hit by a terrible storm." *Storm effect*	(Page 15)
Cue 15	**Ishmael**: ". . . followed by an endless calm . . ." *Fade storm effect, brighten overall lighting*	(**Page 15**)
Cue 16	**Ishmael**: ". . . he had waited for . . ." *Fade Spot on* **Ishmael**	(**Page 15**)
Cue 17	**Ahab**: ". . . but I'll slay him yet!" *Dim overall lighting*	(**Page 15**)
Cue 18	When ready *Bring up Spot on* **Ishmael**	(Page 16)
Cue 19	**Ishmael**: ". . . and waited, patiently." *Fade Spot on* **Ishmael**; *bring up general lighting*	(**Page 16**)
Cue 20	Oaths and cries are heard *Black-out, pause, then up to full for* CURTAIN CALL	(Page 17)

EFFECTS PLOT

Cue 1	When ready *National Anthem played jerkily, followed by introductory music*	(Page 7)
Cue 2	Spot goes out *Sound of tape-recorder being played backwards*	(Page 7)
Cue 3	House Lights come up *Repeat Cue 1*	(Page 7)
Cue 4	**Ishmael:** ". . . the sea . . . the sea . . ." *Short burst of sea noises*	(Page 7)
Cue 5	As **Scarred Seaman** gropes about on floor *Clap of thunder, pause, then exaggerated "thumpbang" to represent **Ahab's** artificial leg*	(Page 9)
Cue 6	**Queequeg** hurls harpoon off stage *Strangled cry, off*	(Page 9)
Cue 7	**Queequeg** and **Ishmael** enter *Music: "Good King Wenceslas"; fade as **Ishmael** starts to speak*	(Page 10)
Cue 8	**Ishmael:** ". . . a lively set of lads." *Sea effects; fade as **Ishmael** begins to speak again*	(Page 12)
Cue 9	**Ishmael:** ". . . heard walking the deck . . ." *"Thump-bang" to represent **Ahab's** artificial leg*	(Page 12)
Cue 10	Crew throw dummy overboard *Loud splash, followed by a cry*	(Page 15)
Cue 11	**Ishmael:** ". . . hit by a terrible storm." *Thunder and lightning*	(Page 15)
Cue 12	**Ishmael:** ". . . followed by an endless calm . . ." *Fade storm*	(Page 15)
Cue 13	**Ahab:** ". . . I'll slay him yet!" *Stirring music to cover scene change*	(Page 16)
Cue 14	The Lights fade *Music swells*	(Page 17)

THE CHERRY SISTERS
FURNITURE AND PROPERTY LIST

On stage: Bench
Several chairs
Table. *On it:* samovar (full of tea), vase
Ball of flowers (for **Basha**)
Flower basket (for **Gnasha**)

Off stage: Bag. *In it:* papers **(Porkin)**
Tray. *On it:* cups and saucers **(Piles)**
Chamber pot **(Stage management)**

Personal: **Footrotski:** watch

LIGHTING PLOT

Property fittings required: nil
Exterior. A veranda or garden

To open: General exterior lighting

Cue 1	**Piles** "dies" by the samovar	(Page 30)
	Fade to Black-out	

EFFECTS PLOT

Cue 1	As CURTAIN rises	(Page 25)
	Music	
Cue 2	**Footrotski** sits down	(Page 25)
	Tree falls	
Cue 3	**Footrotski:** ". . . Moscow, always Moscow."	(Page 25)
	Tree falls	
Cue 4	**Veruka:** ". . . get to Moscow?"	(Page 25)
	Tree falls	

Cue 5	**Basha** and **Veruka** embrace	(Page 26)
	Tree falls	
Cue 6	**Veruka:** ". . . I hate the sight of him!"	(Page 26)
	Horse effect	
Cue 7	**Babuskha** exits	(Page 30)
	Crash of crockery, off	

LAST CALL FOR BREAKFAST
FURNITURE AND PROPERTY LIST

Off stage: Large salt pot **(Stage management)**
Large pepper pot **(Stage management)**

LIGHTING PLOT

Property fittings: nil
A bare stage

To open: Dim lighting

Cue 1	**He** prances towards pepper pot *Black-out*	(Page 37)
Cue 2	As music fades for second time *Bring up Spot on salt pot*	(Page 37)
Cue 3	**She:** ". . . I have become . . ." *Snap out Spot on salt. Bring up Spot on pepper. Pause.* *Snap out Spot on pepper. Bring up Spot on salt again*	(Page 37)
Cue 4	**He:** ". . . move it over there." *Snap out Spot on salt*	(Page 37)
Cue 5	**He:** "Open your legs!" *Bring up Spot uncertainly on pepper then fade. Bring up* *Spot on salt*	(Page 38)
Cue 6	**She:** ". . . darkness . . . dark." *Fade Spot on salt. Bring up Spot down stage on* **Sugar Cube**	(Page 38)
Cue 7	**Sugar Cube:** ". . . separation . . . darkness . . ." *Snap out Spot on* **Sugar Cube**. *Bring up Spot on salt*	(Page 38)
Cue 8	**Sugar Cube** tries to get through Curtain *Bring up House Lights*	(Page 39)

EFFECTS PLOT

Cue 1	As CURTAIN rises Avant-garde *music*	(Page 37)
Cue 2	**Voice** (*off; on echo*): ". . . au petit déjeuner . . . *Train whistle, followed by another burst of* avant-garde *music*	(Page 37)

HENRY THE TENTH
(PART SEVEN)
FURNITURE AND PROPERTY LIST

ACT I

SCENE 1

Off stage: Stick **(Clodpony)**
Thurrible (smoking) **(Priest)**
Coffin **(Soldiers)**

SCENE 2

Off stage: Drum **(Drummer)**

SCENE 3

Off stage: Throne (collapsible) mounted on stage truck **(King)**
Trumpet **(Herald)**

Personal: **Ongar:** Wrist-watch

SCENE 4

Personal: **Wolverhampton:** Sword
Dudley: Sword
Smethwick: Sword

SCENE 5

Off stage: Doll in shawl **(Old Meg)**
Clown's bladder **(Clown)**

ACT II

SCENE 1

Off stage: Drum **(Drummer)**

SCENE 2

On stage: Various trees

Off stage: Trumpet (repaired with handkerchief) **(Herald)**

Personal: **Wolverhampton:** Sword
Dudley: Sword
Smethwick: Sword

SCENE 3

Set: Previous trees in different positions
           small rostrum

Off stage: Dummy soldiers **(Soldiers)**
              Trumpet (shortened) **(Herald)**
              Back of Whale from Moby Dick **(Stage management)**

Personal: **Uxbridge:** Sword
            Amersham: Sword
            Ongar: Sword
            King: Purse of coins

SCENE 4

Strike: Trees
           Rostrum

Off stage: Spears **(Soldiers)**
              Dummy on spear **(Soldier)**
              Trick arrow **(Soldier)**

Personal: **Amersham:** Sword
            Smethwick: Sword
            Uxbridge: Two-handed sword
            Wolverhampton: Two-handed sword
            Dudley: Rope

SCENE 5

Off stage: Stretcher (*see Production Notes, p. 46*) **(Soldiers)**

SCENE 6

Off stage: Doll in shawl **(Old Meg)**
              Trumpet (repaired with handkerchief) **(Herald)**

LIGHTING PLOT

Property fittings required: nil
Various interior and exterior settings

ACT I   Day

To open: General exterior lighting

Cue 1   At end of Scene 1   (Page 48)
            Fade to Black-out, then bring up downstage lighting for
            Chorus

Cue 2   **Chorus** and **Drummer** exit   (Page 49)
            Black-out

Cue 3	When ready	(Page 49)
	Bring up lighting concentrated on central area (where throne should be)	
Cue 4	**Lords** move down stage	(Page 49)
	Gradually bring up overall lighting	
Cue 5	At end of Scene 3	(Page 51)
	Fade to Black-out	
Cue 6	When ready	(Page 51)
	Bring up general lighting	
Cue 7	**All:** ". . . Alack the day."	(Page 55)
	Fade to Black-out	

ACT II Day

To open: Downstage lighting for **Chorus**

Cue 8	**Chorus** and **Drummer** exit	(Page 56)
	Black-out	
Cue 9	When ready	(Page 57)
	Bring up bright overall lighting	
Cue 10	**King** jumps up on rostrum	(Page 58)
	*Bring up Spot on **King***	
Cue 11	**King** exits	(Page 59)
	Fade to Black-out	
Cue 12	When ready	(Page 59)
	Bring up overall lighting for battlefield	
Cue 13	**King:** ". . . all life lay down."	(Page 61)
	Fade to Black-out	
Cue 14	When ready	(Page 62)
	Bring up overall lighting	
Cue 15	**Lords** exit	(Page 62)
	Fade to Black-out, then bring up overall lighting for Scene 6	
Cue 16	**All** (*as they exit*): ". . . Long life to Henry the Eleventh!"	(Page 63)
	*Dim overall lighting, bring up Spot on **Uxbridge***	
Cue 17	**Uxbridge:** ". . . no rest this day."	(Page 63)
	*Start to contract Spot on **Uxbridge**; continue to contract it throughout his speech*	
Cue 18	**Uxbridge:** ". . . while he has life."	(Page 64)
	Snap off Spot	

EFFECTS PLOT

ACT I

Cue 1   As CURTAIN rises   (Page 47)
Funeral bell tolling, solemn music and drums— continue until **Hayseed** *and* **Clodpony** *enter*

Cue 2   At start of Scene 2   (Page 48)
Tucket (*trumpet flourish*) *and drums*

Cue 3   **Herald** raises trumpet to his mouth   (Page 49)
Pause, then blast of sound followed by fanfare

Cue 4   **Herald** raises trumpet   (Page 50)
Fanfare

Cue 5   **Uxbridge:** "My Liege . . ."   (Page 50)
Blast of trumpet, ending abruptly in a screech

Cue 6   At end of Scene 3   (Page 51)
Martial music continue until lights come up for Scene 4

Cue 7   **Herald!** "My Lord . . ."   (Page 52)
Fanfare

Cue 8   At start of Scene 5   (Page 53)
Music for gavotte

Cue 9   (*optional*) **Clown** prepares to sing   (Page 53)
Clown's *song on tape*

Cue 10   **Queen:** ". . . hangs upon the dug."   (Page 53)
Baby crying

Cue 11   **All:** ". . . Alack the day."   (Page 55)
Grim music

ACT II

Cue 12   At start of Scene 2   **(Page 56)**
Bird noises

Cue 13   **Herald** raises trumpet   (Page 57)
Fanfare, followed by snatch of "Hi-ho, hi-ho" *music from* "Snow White"

Cue 14   **Herald** raises trumpet   (Page 58)
Fanfare

Cue 15   At start of Scene 4   (Page 59)
Alarums, excursions, general battle noises

Cue 16   "Dead" **Soldier** crawls off   (Page 60)
Stop battle noises abruptly

Cue 17   **King:** ". . . all life lay down?"   (Page 61)
Music: "I vow to thee my country". *Continue until start of Scene 5*

Cue 18   **Lords** exit   (Page 62)
Sad music—continue until start of Scene 6

Cue 19   **Herald** raises trumpet   (Page 63)
Burst of thunderstorm effect

MADE AND PRINTED IN GREAT BRITAIN BY
LATIMER TREND & COMPANY LTD PLYMOUTH
MADE IN ENGLAND